AF445629

Expose Your Leadership DNA

V.M. Vasudevan

Expose Your Leadership DNA © V. M. Vasudevan 2020
First Edition: January 2020

By ZDP SPECIFICS
ISBN: 978-93-88860-75-8
ZDP Specifics Title : 5

All rights reserved. No part of this publication may be reproduced, stored in a retrieval system, or transmitted, in any form or by any means, electronic, mechanical, photocopying, recording, psychic, or otherwise, without the prior permission of the publishers.

ZDP SPECIFICS
An imprint of Zero Degree Publishing
No.55(7), R Block, 6th Avenue,
Anna Nagar,
Chennai - 600 040

Website: www.zerodegreepublishing.com
E Mail id: zerodegreepublishing@gmail.com
Phone : 98400 65000

Cover Art by Humshini
Typeset by Vidhya Velayudham

FOREWORD

In the world of the digital information highway, books are a relatively the best source of information. There are books and then there are books on leadership. Enough has been written and said about it by, most of them iconic in their pedigree and authored by equally iconic personalities. In this digital noisy arena, not many would have come across a passionate account on leadership that which is influential, inclusive and innovative as V.M. Vasudevan's debut attempt.

The book is very attractive from the angle of its simplicity and as much as it is with the experiential contents. One can thoroughly enjoy the read especially the way the chapters are placed and its relevance to the previous and subsequent chapters are carefully threaded. At the same time, we can pick up the book at any point and continue without having to refer the previous pages and yet understand the big-picture presented.

So what is exactly in this book?

This book on leadership is interspersed with anecdotes and apt references to scriptures with graceful pictorial creativity contributed by his equally talented children – Vikranth and Vismitha. There are many anecdotes from Vasu's own managerial life and a good amount of references to the Bhagwat Gita, Thirupavai & the Thirukural which are very apt to the chapter. There are also numerous references to good selections of the book for each essential skill required for a good leader.

"A leader is one who knows the way, goes the way, shows the way," said John C Maxwell and Vasu has put that to play in this simple and erudite compilation. Much to follow in the same suite, this book has set itself on a path of being amongst the "unputdownable" must-reads.

A journey well begun by Vasu.

Suresh Krishnaswamy
Director- Projects, CTS

CONTENTS

Introduction

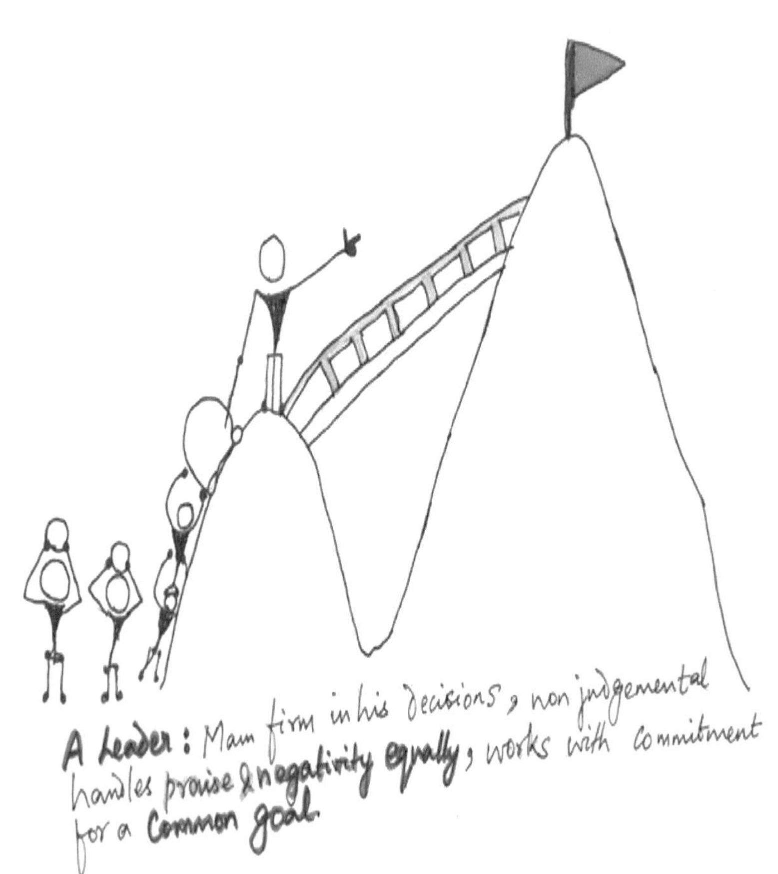

What is leadership?

This sounds like a very easy question and yet it continues to vex a lot of consultants and business leaders. In an effect to answer this, I have tried to define leadership in my own style.

So what exactly is my style?

My approach is to list out what leadership is NOT, and once that list is exhausted what remains should be LEADERSHIP.

The first thing on the list that comes to mind is that leadership has nothing to do with seniority or age. Too many organizations have been operating under the myth that senior executives are good leaders. In reality they are, as their title suggests, just senior executives. Leadership doesn't come with age.

Let me shift focus from the corporate jungle to the cricket grounds for an example. Graeme Smith took on the mantle of captaincy at a little over age 22 with limited prior exposure to international cricket. MS.Dhoni became an example closer to home when he took over as the captain of the Indian T20 team, only to become a benchmark for his and many more generations to come. These examples truly illustrate that age is not a mandate for good leadership.

The second point to note is that leadership has nothing to do with titles. Having a C-Title doesn't make an automatic leader. In fact. I would like to stress on the point that you do not need titles (or hierarchy) to lead.

Thirdly, leadership has nothing to do with personal attributes. The mention of the word "leader" evokes a picture of a grand, domineering and charismatic individual. We are often fixated on iconic historical figures on to whom we attach the attributes of a leader. We don't need extroverted, charismatic traits to practice leadership. And conversely, those with charisma don't automatically lead.

Taking cricket again as an example, there have been leaders like Steven Waugh who would encourage his team to do anything to win (I personally do not align with this form of leadership). There was Imran Khan, who would command his team with a raised voice right in the middle of the playing field and there was Rahul Dravid – silent and yet firm. All of them have been great leaders in their own way.

Finally, to round up the list, leadership is not management. This is a big one. Leadership and management are not synonymous or interchangeable. Say that you have 150 people in your team responsible for P&L. Good for you. need to MANAGE them well. You need to plan, measure, track, monitor, coordinate, solve, hire, mentor, fire etc. In simpler terms, managers MANAGE things while leaders LEAD people.

Heads of political parties in India call themselves leaders, but are actually managers (albeit poor ones in most cases) while Anna Hazare was a leader – one with a vision to lead a captivated nation.

Again we come back to - What is Leadership?

Let me not go further than a scripture that has withstood the test of time in its understanding of and commentary on - the Bhagavat Gita. What does Sri Krishna have to say about the qualities of a leader?

First let me explain the need for a leader to possess the qualities of genuineness and self-righteousness, and then look at what the skills required for a leader are.

यद्यदाचरति श्रेष्ठस्तत्तदेवेतरो जनः |
स यत्प्रमाणं कुरुते लोकस्तदनुवर्तते || 21||
yad yad ācharati śhreshthas tat tad evetaro janah |
sa yat pramānam kurute lokas tad anuvartate || 21||

Whatever "an eminent man" (i.e. one who is famous for his knowledge and work ethics) performs, others with incomplete knowledge will also perform by following his example.

With regard to any duty performed with all its ancillaries by an eminent person, the people with incomplete knowledge will do it with the same ancillaries. Therefore for the protection of the organisation, all acts that are appropriate to each one's role and tasks in the project must always be performed by an eminent person who is distinguished for his wisdom. Otherwise the evil generated from the ruin of the large masses of the organisation will take everyone down.

We are all social animals. We are all imitators too. We form our bedrock of right and wrong from those who we consider models. We try to walk in their footsteps.

People always need a leader who can teach them by example. A leader cannot tell the public to stop smoking if he himself smokes.

The executive head of a state, the father and the school teacher are all assigned leadership roles naturally. All such natural leaders have a great responsibility towards their dependents; therefore they must be conversant with standard books of moral and spiritual codes.

So a great leader should always walk the fine line that upholds high values, morals and ethics at all times.

Having said this, Sri Krishna also elaborates on the skills or qualities that are required from a good leader in Chapter-12.

तुल्यनिन्दास्तुतिर्मौनी सन्तुष्टो येन केनचित् |
अनिकेत: स्थिरमतिर्भक्तिमान्मे प्रियो नर: || 19||

**tulya-nindā-stutir maunī santushto yena kenachit |
aniketah sthira-matir bhaktimān me priyo narah || 19||**

Those who take praise and reproach alike, who are given to silent contemplation, content with what comes their way, without attachment to the place of residence, whose intellect is firmly fixed in Me, and who are full of devotion to Me, such persons are very dear to Me.

These are the qualities that are best suited for a leader – a person who is capable of taking praise and compliments as well as negative feedback and blame with equanimity, who can remain silent when in judgement, whose decision making is very clear and firm, who is not attached to a place (or project or title) and works with full devotion on a common goal.

This may sound easy on a first reading but let us dive into this with greater depth and detail. How easy is it for anyone to have an equipoise for honour and dishonour? It is not very easy to take both honour and dishonour with the same feeling by oneself. Only great leaders have displayed the ability to keep their cool in case of the latter.

Crows and swans make diametrically opposite choices. While crows are drawn to garbage piles, the majestic swans are attracted by tranquil lakes. Similarly the minds of the common people are drawn towards materialistic and non-productive content. The leaders possess visionary minds, and thus worldly talks seem as attractive to them as a pile of garbage. This is what is meant by silent contemplation.

To draw corporate parallels, 'without attachment to a place' refers to any single organization or post. A leader views all jobs as temporary tasks, with the permanent value being attached to the universal goal of SUCCESS FOR ALL.

Why many of us are attracted to become a leader?

I did a causal sweep across the globe to list the top few reasons that people want to become a leader. What I found was the following, which I has listed under the sub-categories of wrong and right:

Wrong reasons:

• **Money**

Money is nice, no arguments. And many of the highest paid positions come with a leadership role. But if all you want is a bigger paycheck, you're on the wrong track.

• **Power**

Power means making the difficult decisions. Power means being the one to determine when employees are fired or laid off. It means disappointing and upsetting people on a regular basis. Does that sound like fun? It isn't.

• **Prestige**

Being a leader can come with some nice perks. People tend to be polite to you. You might get the nicer room at the hotel or, depending on your company, the bigger office. But if you're like most good leaders you'll spend little of your time luxuriating in these fringe benefits, and a lot of it worrying about the results you're trying to achieve. This, too, is a lots less fun than it looks.

Right reasons:

• **Responsibility**

If you want to drive a common goal of success and steer a group of people towards that, it certainly calls for greater responsibility. Responsibility comes with hard work and skill. If these skills are innate in you, you know what you should do.

• People

Great leaders often put a lot of time and effort into improving other people and helping them become more successful by giving constructive and positive feedback, and identifying the right resources that will support their growth. If this sounds relatable, then you are fit for a leadership position.

• Broad vision

If you have a dream of you can't achieve without the help of others, you'll need leadership skills to get them behind you. Having a mission for your team or organization is the best reason there is for wanting to be a leader.

There are certain events or situations that could create a leader within you. They are:

1. Turbulent times

2. When faced against the wall

3. A ship with no one to steer and direct

4. High risk with high gain

5. A strong backing of your friends

What is required to be a great leader?

I would like to refer to the quote from Dr. Martin Luther King Jr.

"If a man is called to be a street sweeper, he should sweep streets even as a Michelangelo painted, or Beethoven composed music or Shakespeare wrote poetry. He should sweep streets so well that all the hosts of heaven and earth will pause to say, 'Here lived a great street sweeper who did his job well."

This quote summarizes the exact skill required to become a great leader. Since not everyone is born a Michelangelo or a Shakespeare, I have created an apt acronym that summarizes what is needed to become either.

I call it the **IMAGE** – **I**magination **M**astery **A**uthentic **G**enerous **E**thics

See yourself in the mirror and the image should be of a leader which is yourself.

Imagination: From meeting to meeting, from flight to taxi, from bus to tube, from emails to conference calls - the fast paced life we live is draining us of our energy, hunger and most importantly an imagination. The reality is that unless we create something successfully in our minds first, it is nigh on impossible to achieve it in reality.

Mastery: Self-mastery is being in control of the internal thought processes that guide your emotions, habits, and behaviors. A leader is looked up to on multiple levels – physical, mental, observational and even abstract - and hence mastering the self is very important.

Authentic: Leaders give it their all to to overcome their own fears and use their strengths to the maximum. Authentic refers to truthful intent form the heart. Leaders are not afraid to dig deep, lead with courage and are be empathetic - all of which only come from listening to the heart.

Generous: When we think of generosity, our thoughts automatically drift to gifts of money or charity. In the context of leadership, there are other gifts that don't have a monetary value, but whose value is beyond measure. These include giving someone a chance; giving someone the benefit of the doubt; and giving others a reason to want to work for you. It entails giving others latitude, permission to make mistakes, and providing them with all the information that they need to do the job. It's giving them the authority that goes with responsibility – it's giving them due credit for their ideas.

Ethics: Ethical leaders do the right thing, at the right time, for the right reasons. They put their ethics before the bottom line – and research shows that this makes it more likely their teams will be loyal, dedicated and ethical in return.

These are few other skills that I have collected from the internet

• Patience

• Empathy

• Active listening

• Reliability

• Dependability

• Creativity

• Positivity

• Effective feedback

• Timely communication

• Team building

• Flexibility

• Risk-taking

• Ability to teach and mentor

How to determine if you are a leader in the making?

Whenever I introduce myself as an executive coach, listeners often assume that that I coach only C-suite or higher level executives in that food chain. Rarely do I find people who look at themselves as a leader or potential leader. If what John Maxwell (author of the book The 21 Irrefutable Laws of Leadership) said is true, if leadership is only influence, nothing more nothing less - than many of them are deceiving themselves.

So the question isn't "Are we leaders?" Yes, we are all. We lead in some way or fashion in the five circles of influence (self, family, team, organization, community). A better question would be "What kind or type of leader are we?"

There is a short way to find out about the leader inside of you and I call this method as **DNA** – **D**iscover, **N**urture & Assess. Like the acronym, the leadership DNA is within you and all you have to do is to look inwards to find it.

Leadership Framework

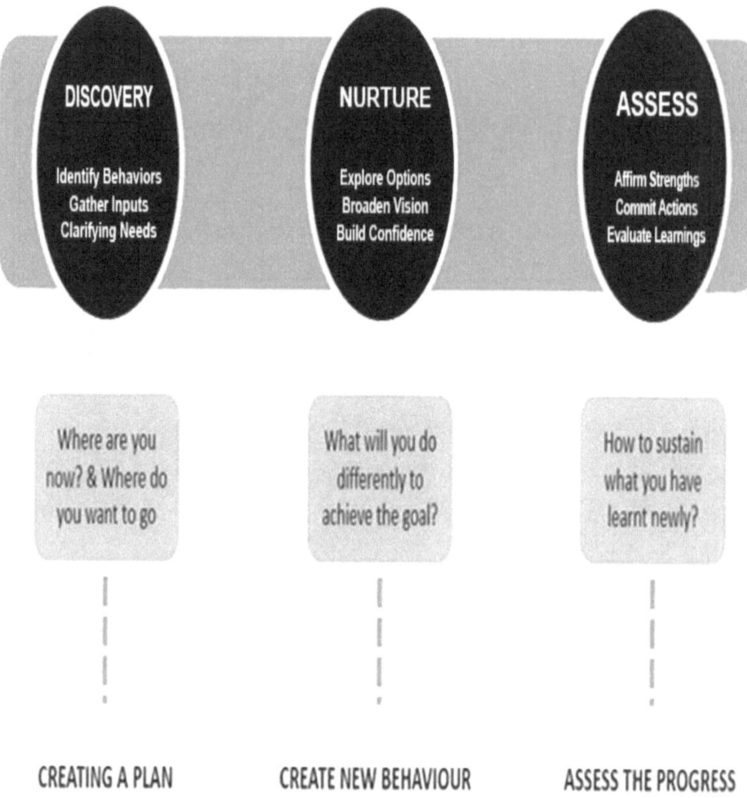

Leadership Abilities

The world does not divide its members into the categories of leaders and followers. It how we define or slot ourselves based on our innate actions. We are sometimes scared to exhibit or traits of leadership and often believe that we do not possess them at all. This is a gross mistake many of us (parents, teachers, managers, consultants) often make.

The next mistake many of us make is that we assume that there is space only for one leader – and by default everyone else has to be a follower. This is a typical misconception perpetrated by the corporate hierarchy. I want to challenge this assumption. Why can't there be multiple leaders in teams? Most teams performed better with multiple leaders.

There is a lot of literature today about how the world needs more leadership from more places: it needs for more people to step up and lead. So, we need to be watchful about our (inaccurate) beliefs about leadership.

So what are the salient characteristics a leader need to display?

Many studies have come to the conclusion that qualities people associate with a leader are: Sensitivity, Intelligence, Dedication, and Dynamism.

Does it occur to you that all these 4 qualities are certainly inside of you? I have developed a model that will help you unearth each of these traits and take a step forward towards. This is my theory that leadership skill is already inside of everyone. For many display them and for those who do not they need to be nurtured and they too become leaders. So I developed a model which will help everyone to become a better leader from where they were.

My model is a 'Win-Win' kind and is driven by "Satisfaction". This model works under the assumption that everyone has leadership skill buried inside of them and they have not made the effort to identify and nurture it till now. The trouble is more cultural than individual. One most important elephant in the room that prevents potential leaders form accepting their ability is the fear of responsibility.

Right from primary school days, we are made to fear leadership by making sound like a monstrous and impossible undertaking.. Yes, it is a tough one but instead of scaring our young friends, why not show them the way to do it right? This is missing in our education system today. We do not build leaders in our schools and colleges – you only think of it during the post-graduation stage. This needs to change if we need more leaders.

Leadership Model

My model is aptly named DNA i.e. Discovering-Nurturing-Assessing:

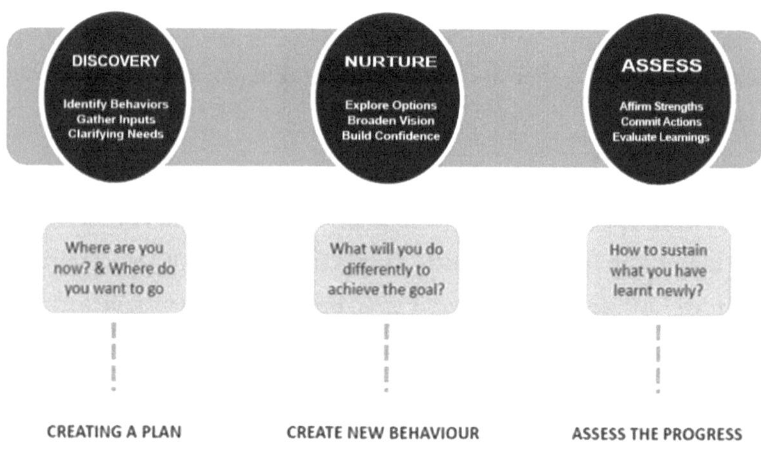

The core concept of this model we need a mentor to germinate our inherent skill (strand 1) we need to leverage our latent learning capabilities (strand 2). When these strands interlock to form a double helix, the message transfer for developing, enhancing and functioning are the best as found in nature.

Leadership is not about individual victory but collectively victory of the team. It is not an individual race but a relay. Nature has its own way of showing this example – take the mango, coconut and jasmine plant. All of them have a separate calling and do not aspire to compare their performance (Length of the tree, fruit production) or strength of the tree (ability to withstand hurricanes) with others. Likewise each human also has a unique space and role to play in the cosmos. True inner fulfillment will emerge only when we have found this place and have mastered the art of contentment, love and calm.

I have also divided the book into 3 sections namely – Discovery, Nurturing & Assessment. In the discovery section I have tried to elaborate on specific leadership topics such as how a leader should think, how he questions data, what should he do to be successful.In the second section on Nurturing I try to explain how you can nurture certain leadership qualities such as being efficient, connecting with people, overcoming certain negative contents etc.. I am using this section mainly to illustrate what resolution process a leader must use to tackle common situations.

In the final section of the book which is called Assessment, I have tried to give some practical steps or tips to handle common shortcomings we all possess. For example, how to de-stress yourself, how to take responsibility for collective failures etc. This section is the shortest section of the book as the assessment process is more personal and case-based, and thus the onus is on your mentor or an executive coach to assess and guide you forward. I have provided you with a succinct sample to get started.

I request you, my readers, to apply this model to any facet of your daily life - discover what your desire is, nurture the solution to achieve and assess your progress.

I guarantee you that your possible problems, issues, bucket list entries and new habits will be a new lease of life. .

Prepare yourself to go one this life changing journey and we will meet at the end.

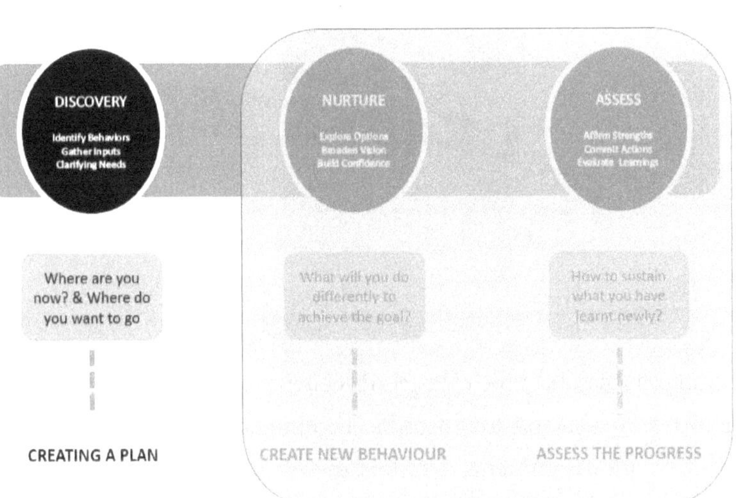
DISCOVERY
Identify Behaviors
Gather Inputs
Clarifying Needs

NURTURE
Explore Options
Broaden Vision
Build Confidence

ASSESS
Affirm Strengths
Commit Actions
Evaluate Learnings

Where are you now? & Where do you want to go

What will you do differently to achieve the goal?

How to sustain what you have learnt newly?

CREATING A PLAN

CREATE NEW BEHAVIOUR

ASSESS THE PROGRESS

Leadership Explained in 6 words

The first successful trait of a good leader is the ability to take tough decisions or work on tough tasks. To emulate this, I wanted to start with a tough assignment. I tasked myself with explaining leadership in only 6 words and 6 sentences.

Why did I settle on 6 words? Let me contextualize before getting into the actual explanation.

During an instance, science fiction author Aruther C. Clarke recounts: While having lunch with his friends at a restaurant, Ernest Hemingway bets the table $10 each that he can pen an entire self-explanatory story in only 6 words. After the pot is assembled, Hemingway writes "For Sale: Baby shoes, never worn" on a napkin, passes around the table and collects his winnings.

The concept of trying to tell a story using an absolute minimum word count is generally known as flash fiction. This literary form of fiction with brevity is now accepted within 1000 words. There also exists a concept called micro fiction which allows a limit of 100 words. The same concept holds true for micro blogs such as Twitter.

Hemingway himself arrived at the six word limitation based on the concept of Six-Word Memoirs. I was unaware of this until a few months back when stumbled upon it during a search for some good short stories. This inspired me to write about leadership based, beginning with the task to explain leadership using this concept.

Here are my 6-point musings on **LEADERSHIP**:

1. **It's more than money and power**

2. **Determination is critical for self-satisfaction**

3. **Passion is really all that matters**

4. **Being challenged everyday makes you happier**

5. **You are clueless without direction**

6. **Less advice, More commitment, Share results**

These are the others which I coined, of course while gazing at the ceiling, and it was worth the gazing.

1   .

Opportunities don't wait, just take it

We all wait for opportunities to invite us but the reality is, we have to find opportunities. We always wait to get better things in life. Nothing comes without putting in the effort. Often, we're given chances but we don't recognize them for what they are. Maintain the focus, and good things will start to happen.

2.

Stay patient, trust your instincts throughout

Don't let things get on your nerves. Just be patient, and relax. You have to trust yourself and the things you are doing. It does take time. When it gets tough, you have to be strong and calm.

3.

Keep moving, you'll get there finally

Just be steady, stay focused and stick to the path you are on, and you are sure to see the light of hope. Trust yourself if you are on the right track. It may take long, but you will surely get there.

4.

Work like deadline is tomorrow

No delay. No regrets. Nothing assures you that you will have a better tomorrow. Each day has something different to offer. Work every day to the fullest so that you don't regret the time that was wasted.

5.

Big things often have small beginnings

Don't worry if it is a small beginning. You never know what mega-stardom might be in store. Many times, making big changes while staying true to the small beginnings lead to   spectacular outcomes.

6.

Always remember that everyone struggles

The grass is always greener on the other side. Never think that only you are undergoing stress, bad moments, mediocre decisions, and risky actions. Everyone has, is or will go through it too.

7.

When nothing goes right, turn left

Stop chasing the same path over and over again If it isn't working, you need to look at other options. Maybe 'left' will not take you to the destination, but at-least takes you a step forward and presents the problem from a different angle.

8.

Don't be busy, be more productive

Don't try to work harder, you need to work smarter. Remember success comes only to those who are smarter and more productive. Not to those who are constantly busy.

9.

Keep forgetting what you're angry about

Anger will kill your mind. The best cure for anger is forgetfulness. Never let anger remain in your mind for more than 5 minutes – try it and you will feel the change.

10.

Done is better than chasing perfection

If time permits, you can try to perfect the solution. But first you need a working solution. So remember not to chase perfection from the start, et. an initial result and then try for perfection. Sometimes, 'too perfect' may not be the desired result (that is the reason we have spouses.)

Finally on a lighter note, since I also belong to this fraternity of leadership:

You're absolutely unique, just like everybody

Having got to know about leadership and some of its characteristics many of us now would want to try it and experience success. Everyone wants to win and enjoy the nectar called SUCCESS but not many of them know how it is done.

Success is based totally on the mindset. What better way to know how it is done than by looking into the minds of the champions. Are you ready?

Dive into the champion's mind, see how it works

Everyone wants to win, to be a champion and to succeed. But they don't know how or even where to start. For a holistic view, let us look at the 'whys' first before taking the "how" angle.

Whenever someone says something nice about you, you immediately feel joy, your esteem builds and the general atmosphere becomes light and enjoyable. If you achieve something great or win a competition, the number of people praising you increases, thereby causing these feelings to increase exponentially as well. Your mind registers this moment forever. The memory of this makes you want this feeling every time - thus making winning addictive.

So why do we want this addiction?

Firstly, we are all born to win. We have a primal instinct that compels us to achieve. That drive is what is behind each and every thought and action of ours. It's what initiates every moment of our lives. Have you ever heard anyone say they can't wait to get up the next day to fail? All we ever hear is how tired people are while chasing their preconceived goals and how much they want to succeed and get fulfillment from their actions. Never do we find anyone who enjoys failures (except the match fixers in cricket).

If we forego the pursuit of our goals and ambitions, it is equivalent to turning our backs on our inborn talents and the privilege of life. Therefore it is imperative that we all win and succeed. This answers the 'why' so now let us head to the 'how'.

Is it safe for me to presume that you also want to be a champion?

Well, I have some good news and some bad news for you. The good news is that sports psychologist Dr. Jim Afremow has written a book called "The Champion's Mind: How Great Athletes Think, Train and Thrive" which breaks down the mental strategies that many sports champions use to excel on the field. The bad news is that you have to read it fully - I'm still halfway only through the book so I cannot furnish the full contents.

Here anyway is the gist of what I understood so far: To start with, you must realize that nobody has a "Champion" gene. Champions are not born - they become one. So you must empower your mind with the truth that anybody can become a champion. How? You need to think like them, you need to practice like them and you need to act like them.

So how do they think?

1. Champions Expect To Win: Weather they walk onto to the court, a field, into a meeting room or an examination, they always expect to win. They always aim for GOLD. Settling for silver is out of the question. In fact they are surprised when they don't win. They have a strong belief that positive thinking and actions will lead them to the result. They win in their minds first, then they win the hearts of the opponents, fans or customers.

From recent times, the Australian cricket team is the best example for this tip. Right from their captain Kim Huges in the late 70s to today's Steve Smith & Tim Paine, they share a similarity in leadership characteristics – a strong mind that is very positive even in adverse conditions. Kim started it, Allan Border nurtured it, Steve Waugh refined it, Ricky Pointing perfected it and Michael Clark executed it beyond perfection. There have been many instances where everyone in the stadium other than these captains would have accepted that defeat was inevitable, only for the team to emerge victorious at the end.

2. Champions Celebrate Even The Small Wins: By celebrating small wins, they reiterate in their mind the confidence to go for the next big win. Remember that a marathon always begins with a successful first kilometer. A really big win is in fact an accumulation of many smaller wins. One cautionary note is that while celebrating wins, we should not become complacent but instead be motivated to reach higher, further and faster.

The two persons who come to my mind who embody this are Anil Kumble & Muttaih Muralitharan. They celebrated every win uproariously but also celebrated the beautiful deliveries that inhibited the batsmen (the small wins). These childlike celebrations for small moments were what that took them to 600 test wickets and beyond.

3. Champions Don't Make Excuses When They Don't Win: It is difficult when you lose and you may want to blame something or someone, but champions never blame others for the loss but turn the focus inwards towards their own faults. They always introspect on how they can do better. They view their defeats as opportunities to grow.

Every sports athlete qualifies for this tip, but I would like to specially call out Sachin Tendulkar's 241 in the Sydney test during the 2003-2004 Australian tour. Before this test, the scores of the master blaster were - 0, DNB, 1, 37, 0, 44 with a paltry average of 16.4. His dismissals were caught in the offside field. Critics started to write off Tendulkar's technique and declared that it was an end of his era. Many of his followers were also worried, but Tendulkar was not. Nor did he ever blame the pitch, situation or anything else but himself. He introspected on his errors, and came back stronger than ever with scores of 241 & 60 (not out).

4. Champions Focus on What They GET To Do, Not What They HAVE To Do: They see their work as a joyful journey and not as a mere obligation to get things done. They know that if they want to win, they need to appreciate the thorny path of success. They may not like the work, schedule or approach but their attitude and will-power helps them overcome this negative inclination.

Novak Djokovic is a wonderful example of this. Hailing from Serbia, a country with minimal tennis training and infrastructure, Novak's sheer love for the game kept him going. His first few years as a pro yielded nothing further than losses in the third round of the main slams. This did not deter him from his goal to lift the championship trophy. In 2007 Rogers Cup in Montreal, he defeated No. 3 Andy Roddick in the quarterfinals, No. 2 Nadal in the semi-finals, and No. 1 Federer in the finals. This was the first time a player had defeated the top three ranked players in one tournament since Boris Becker in 1994. All these victories stemmed from his appreciation for what he GOT to do, not what he HAD to do.

5. Champions Believe They Will Experience More Wins in the Future: Their faith is greater than their fears. Their positive attitude is greater than the chorus of negative elements around them. Their passion for the task is greater than the challenges they face. In spite of the situation they are in, they always believe that the best days are ahead of them and not behind them. Roger Federer is the best example for this tip.

After his loss to Djokovic in the Paris Masters semi-finals, Federer said in his post-match "Losing is never fun so that's why I guess I have this face right now. There's only so much you can do, the opponent is slightly better than you on that day. Overall I'm happy with my game. I'm looking forward to a rest now and good preparation in the next few months" – I rest my case.

Want to test if you are also a champion? Let us take a quick review:

• If you can spot greatness in someone else, then you already have some of that greatness within you, because only a person with similar traits can recognize those in others

• The mental abilities of confidence, concentration, and composure are crucial for being a champion in everything you undertake

•Champions aren't made in gyms. Champions are made from something they have deep inside them – a desire, a dream, and a vision

• Train like you are No.2, but compete like you are No. 1

• It takes more than 10 years or even longer to become an overnight success

• Just like how a stand-up comedy is rehearsed for more than 10 times, the finals of the tournament are also rehearsed in the mind and practice sessions.

We have had a fair idea of how the champions think but they also mould their mental setup. How? Here are some of the tools they use:

The tools are:

1. Technical: Their mechanics, their coordination.

2. Tactical: The strategies they use to outmaneuver their opponent on the court, field, etc.

3. Physical: Strength, stamina and conditioning.

4. Mental: – Their thoughts, their feelings, their emotions.

Now that you know the secret, the next thing to tackle is. You need to keep doing this everyday, 24/7. Let me try and make it a bit easier by saying that to start with, try taking baby steps such as working on each of the points one by one till they get imbibed into your work-schedule. Then move on to the next and slowly, over time, you will involuntarily start to function as a champion.

Most of the points articulated in this chapter may have already reached you (or been conveyed) as leadership advice but what you may not know is how you can take these tips from intent to reality to become a champion in real life.

There are certain self-skills that we are aware of but are not using. It is very imperative that you are not only aware, but you also leverage them to mould you into a champion. How? Let's look at that in the next chapter.

Break the rules whenever possible

Breaking the rules - Creativity and Management

There is substantial knowledge buried deep inside our brain that we do not want to use for some reasons unknown. Only when we decide to make a conscious effort to change do we notice that the tools for change have been present with us the whole time. This kind of information is stored in two regions: the short term and the long term memory.

The short term memory is like making one of many possible chess moves, or remembering a hotel room number. These are processed in the front of the brain in a highly developed area called the prefrontal lobe. Recollection is translated into long-term memory in the hippocampus, an area in the deeper brain. Hippocampus takes simultaneous memories from different sensory regions of the brain and connects them into a single "episode" of memory. For example, you may have one memory of a dinner party rather than multiple separate memories of how the party looked, sounded or smelled.

In addition to these 2 memory regions, we also have a kind of thinking called 'assumptions'. Now the question is - why do we assume things?

Let's say that as I type this paragraph, I decide to take a short break and come back. In doing so, I am under the assumption that the keyboard would be still there, the PC will be in hibernate mode and the mouse by the right side. Why am I assuming this? Our assumptions are based on past experience, knowledge of how things work, memory, inferences, observations and imagination.

All leaders have some beliefs or assumptions about their leadership skills and abilities. Rarely have I seen or heard anyone publicly proclaim his own greatness in leadership. Then one day a person named David Burkus comes and turns my beliefs upside down …

Caution: He is a very dangerous man …

He has punctured two of my long-standing beliefs in Creativity & Management.

I used to be under the impression that I was, by nature, not a creative person and hence was absolved of all responsibility to be creative. Then I read his book Myths of Creativity, and now I can no longer sit on the couch complacently with potato chips watching T20 cricket and saying "I am not the creative type, it doesn't run in my genes".

He states in this book that the truth about creativity, innovation, and great ideas are already inside us. However, we always fall prey to myths that have been perpetuated over millennia and fail to act on our ideas, which ultimately wither and die.

The second myth Burkus busted through his new book on management - Under New Management - on the efficacy (or lack thereof) of old management and leadership practices. We intuitively understand that they are long past their sell-by date, but allow them to continue nonetheless.

Some radical approaches his book covers includes:

- Banning emails

- Eliminating managers

- Making salaries transparent

- Abandoning open-office layouts

- Putting customers second.

Although these may sound crazy, counterintuitive or sometimes fanciful, all of the new approaches presented by the author have been successfully implemented in the current corporate world. Eliminating managers is one of the most surprising concepts, yet it has worked wonders for cases like that of start-up Valve Software (valued at 4 billion USD), where teams are driven by the realization that no one will tell them what to do.

There is specific content in Burkus's book like "Ditch the appraisal system", "Throw the bell-curve out", "Pay People to Quit," or my favourite one "Fire the Manager" [I can see my entire product team nodding their heads].

which clearly addresses some of all our frustrations with long-standing business practices, l… But that's not the point I'm trying to make.

What the book prescribes is a systematic and joyful change from WHAT WAS to create WHAT SHOULD BE, by considering the hard truth:

We just may be part of the problem, rather than part of the solution …

Many of us may have advocated these changes in tea-time conversations, but we are not yet ready for implementing the change ourselves. Many of us worry that it is difficult to change the system, or that we are too powerless in the hierarchy, or that there is too much politics we don't have the firepower to clean up. We all start but worry if we can go the distance.

Let us try to find some realistic solutions. Three quick questions came to my mind as well as to many acquaintances who have read the book. All of them were based on the assumption that the changes elaborated in the book are generally valid and desired. [Note: I add another assumption that you are in a position to take business/operational decisions]

1. Why haven't I implemented all these ideas?

If we are all honest to ourselves, most of these changes are long-overdue and well-known to all of us. So we have to consider the reasons for not having made the leap years ago. Job security, fear of the unknown, lack of support. The reasons and excuses are many.

Knowing why we have not changed prepares us TO change. This is the first thought process that a leader should start with. Having known the mindset changes required to be a champion, our first step should be that we should make ourselves ready for the change. Once this question arises, a true leaders who are will only be able to live with himself they get the clarity on the readiness to change.

2. How have I personally helped maintain the status quo, rather than support needed changes?

Most of us are aware that any change that we do will create an entry into the RISK register. Sometimes it is a known and manageable one but many times it is unknown. This uncertainty creates a lingering doubt in our decision-making system. Having said this, another point which I like to make is that the current 'Generation Z' is of the belief that the option involving greater risk has the highest payoff.

Let's play a game. Let's flip a coin. If heads comes up, I'll pay you Rs.150. If tails comes up, you lose Rs.100. Is this a game you want to play? If you decide to play the game only once, your answer will be NO. Let me change the stakes – instead of 100 & 150 let me make it Rs.10,000/= and Rs.15,000/=. You will now run 150Kms from the location gasping for breath.

Why? The general human tendency is to be loss-averse. So without complete comprehension, we usually act in ways that either actively or tacitly support the status quo. Why should we get into risky situations when there are other social and peer pressures on our shoulders? If we are required to change and help others change, we have to identify these situations and make different choices.

When we decide to change our choices, we change the outcomes naturally.

3. What do I need to do now to change this?

Burkus gives some good general directions on how to effect changes of this magnitude, but we still need to drill down changes at personal level before we can support and create the larger changes.

The 'before we can change a system, we have to change ourselves' theory of Burkus echo's Gandhi's famous "Be the change you want see". Gandhi has actually even listed 7 fundamentals that he prescribes for changing a system:

1. Change Yourself

2. You are in control

3. Forgive and let go

4. You will not move without any action

5. Feel the present

6. Persistence

7. See good in people and help them.

Burkus has elaborated pretty similar concepts from Western philosophy while I prefer to stay with our Indian culture.

Change can be good and change is needed, but we have to prepare ourselves to choose our change roles wisely. Real change requires more preparation than thinking about and answering a few questions in your mind. However, you probably have already had some experience doing this.

The bottom line is that it is not enough to know which tool will enhance you but you should also be equipped to choose the right change and use the right tool at the right time. This requires immense planning, time and practice which the real world does not offer to us very easily.

Many times in your life, you will feel stuck at a level or place and would want to move ahead. You may want to get yourself out of the shackles and run ahead. You will have lots of options, choices and thoughts in your head. Even if there is no need for change, a leader's mind is still occupied with several thoughts - distracting him from his end goal. This brings us to the next logical question that leaders may have – "I have interests in multiple avenues, which one should I focus on first?"

Is Multi-Potential An Issue?

Cannot Focus on One thing - What to do?

"The true secret of happiness lies in taking a genuine interest in all the details of daily life." - *William Morris*

Time is linear and it is equal to all. The janitor has 24 hours so as the CEO. An architect baker, mason, musician, a cat sitting on the sofa... each of them have the same 24 hours. Each one of them could also have multiple interests and passions - be it arts, photography, academic or anything else. So the question is, how can they make all of this fit into the magic number of 24 hours?

The reason we as humans have multiple interests is because of how nature has wired us. There is a principle called "The Bumblebee principle" which explains why we should refuse to confine ourselves to an interest. The bee begins its journey to collect nectar from a flower. Once it has finished with the flower, it flies to the next one and the process keeps repeating.

As humans, we are also programmed to work this way. We embark on an activity or task because we want the 'nectar' from it. Once we have got it, we move on to the next task. What determines the end of this search depends on that person's need and satisfaction. Once the reward is obtained, the search ends.

People have different thresholds and varying degrees of focus. Distraction is the main differentiator between winners and losers. How soon you get distracted gives an accurate picture of how far can you go in a task which requires undivided focus.

There are also other kinds of people.

Are you a person who gets multiple inspiring ideas every day? Do you wake up, energized with such thoughts, only to end the day dejected because you did not act on them?

You are not alone. I am like that as well and there are many others in this community. This feeling does create doubt about weather being a jack-of-all-trades is a good thing after all. But, there is a 'but'.

Let me welcome you to the world of the 'multipotentialite', a word I first came across in a TEDx Talk by Emilie Wapnick (TEDx April 2015). Who exactly is a Multipotentialite?

What is Multipotentialites?

The English dictionary defines it as "somebody who has potential in multiple fields." Sounds cool, right? The first time i heard this, I was skeptical if this was indeed a useful thing that adds value to your life or career?

The dictionary goes on to explain how multipotentialites do not bore easily as their varied interests means that something will always catch their fancy. Unfortunately, it doesn't work that way. And I say this from experience.

I am an electronic software engineer who started out as a telecommunication specialist, then moved on to the e-Commerce payments field to a failed entrepreneurial stint and moved on to agile coaching. As of today, I want to be an author - a famous author. I haven't stuck to any particular field, so I cannot call myself an expert or a specialist—words the corporate world loves. Each of the switches in my career path have taken place on losing interest in each particular domain, and this process is repeating. I detest groups that talk about promotions and success in life since I am struggling to find my passion here. I instead talk about new beginnings. But it is difficult to navigate the corporate world with this stance. It's not easy to explain that you have multiple interests and a single one cannot sustain your focus. At every appraisal cycle, managers who leverage multipotentialites to firefight multiple situations block their progress up the corporate ladder stating this very trait, alluding to a 'lack of domain expertise'.

Without a supportive environment, several things can go wrong. Here are some of them.

1. Great Ideas but no tangible output

Sometime you may get so many ideas that it is hard to pick one to execute. Sometimes you may also doubt your ability to take the idea to completion. Sometimes you have a desire to executing multiple ideas at a time and sometimes you want to drop it all things and go to bed.

Even specialists get into this mode, but they a strong pull towards one line of thought which pulls them back on track. It is people who do not have that one single thread who are left alone in the middle, dangling.

2. Getting tagged with the "Irresponsible" or "Careless" label

You may begin to feel like you are an irresponsible person because you don't stick to anything for too long. You lack the commitment of an 'expert' which could only mean a lack of responsibility and carelessness. [Do keep in mind that I am not trying to rationalize real laziness/ carelessness as being a multipotentialite]

In the corporate context, it is important to understand that multipotentialites like this need to be rotated while being assigned tasks, and not asked to do repetitive work. Otherwise there is a high likelihood of being boxed into these labels.

3. Blame game

You may start to think that it is all your fault. You may feel that there is something is wrong in the way you perform. You start to analyze yourself at a micro level. You might try to analyze why you can't be as serious as your peers. You might also hear a lot of the "discipline is the missing link' school of advice .

Your mind is not willing to listen to the fact that you have completed a task and are just looking for an outlet in the form of a new one.

4. Disappointment lingers

You are unable to come up with a concrete goal since your interests/ passions keep varying. You know that you are capable of putting all the efforts into a goal, yet the end point does not bring joy to you. Even if some of the tasks are done on time with perfection, and aesthetics it does not deliver fulfillment. The goal constantly wants to change and this leads to an erosion of self-confidence.

Happiness in general can be elusive even for the richest or most successful person. And for people with different passions, it is that much more stressful.

5. The Pyramid

You keep searching for life's purpose or singular goal that will make you a full person. You always tend to feel that there is something out there which you are not being able to find. Something which you can settle down with. It can be and must be found only by you. After finding it, getting there will be another treacherous path. Beware: This path is full of lies.

Chances are you are like me and have no clue what you want to do. It is a struggle almost every adult goes through. "What do I want to do with my life?" The simple answer to this is in the Bhagvat Gita, in the chapter on Karma yoga. You are part of this cosmic system to perform your duties – do not worry about the fruits of it or finding the WHY.

6. Clueless

You are unsure of your strengths and weaknesses. You seem to be drifting the vast ocean in search of solid ground. Attending seminars and reading motivational books does not serve the purpose. Workshops and seminars are basically financial speed dating for the clueless.

But let us look at the flip side. Politicians today are more worried about losing touch with their constituencies and afraid of losing elections, but are blissful in ignorance about their government's failure to fix real issues. So being clueless might not be so bad after all.

7. Suppression

You suppress your natural behaviour and try to stick to a goal even if it is going to kill you. You try to keep reiterating that things will work out in the end. In reality, you feel a void.

This is the world of a multipotentialite in a nutshell.

Even with all these negative influences, multipotentialites can get a lot of things done. They have 3 big advantages which are (1) Idea Synthesis, (2) Quick Learning and (3) Adaptability.

In a team they are the ones who come up with innovative ideas. What they lack is a belief in the self. A quote by Katie Kacvinsky sums what needs to be done. She says, "You need to be content with small steps. That's all life is. Small steps that you take every day so when you look back down the road it all adds up and you know you covered some distance." When you have hundreds of things that you would like to do, it helps to make a list. Write down your desires and start with one of them. That's it. Don't expect anything and be content with the desire to learn.

When you feel saturated, stop and proceed to do the next thing on your list. The list will grow and so will you. Drop the expectations that you need to finish the project. It's the learning that counts for you. So choose to focus on your strengths. Success will surely follow. The only caveat is that you must never leave the core task (which brings you money or satisfaction) astray. The core task should always be done and you can express you multipotentialite personality outside of that.

Now that you have some understanding of how to handle multiple interest that you have, you need to move on. The next possible and more logical awareness has to be questioning yourself. Which path do I take? Which item from my laundry list should I start with first?

Even the question needs to be specifically directed. This type of questioning is called "Powerful Questioning".

"The question is not who is going to let me; it's who is going to stop me"–*Ayn Rand.*

Leaders ask the wrong questions all the time. We ask questions that drain our energy, lead to dead ends, limit our options, or trap us in a box. So what do good or great leaders do in this situation?

They ask questions which will inspire minds, engage the team, lead to new options and better solutions. This is the next item to be discussed in this book.

How do you feel about moving on?

Powerful Questioning: What & How to enhance it?

There is a very old saying - "the curiosity kills the cat". This may be true but in today's corporate world, it enlivens the leaders. The power of asking questions is also tied to the idea of curiosity. Why? Curious people — who tend to ask more questions about the process, expectation and broader purpose — are more comfortable with ambiguity. Modern business structures are now built largely on ambiguity. We need to be adept with this changing ecosystem and advancing technology.

If you want to be a successful leader or manager, you need more than questioning skills - you need powerful questioning skills. In order to do this, you need to first:

Stop giving advices (free once immediately)

Ask, do not direct

Listen more (80% listening, 20% talking)

Before moving any further, let us explore how the human brain is naturally wired.

The brain naturally goes in search of an answer when it is posed with a question. The direction that the search takes depends very much on how the question is prosed (appropriately or not), when it is posed (getting the timing right), and the actual type of question. There is an indirect subtext which defines the tone. (I can see the male fraternity nodding purely thinking of their spouses. CLAP-CLAP)

From this, we are able to perceive that there are a lot of parameters that makes a question a truly good one. It's no longer just about the content but also about all the adjectives that surrounds them. This includes the timing, the tone and modulation, the pauses between the words or phrases and the body language.

There are many times where leaders assume that they know more than the person standing in front of them. So how should we ask questions? Before answering this, there is something else we need to know first.

Why do we need to question?

This need comes from the fact that the human brain always grapples with the need to suppress anxiety by seeking answers, sometimes even to the unknown. When you need to take a big decision in your life, you naturally a sense of anxiety. This is the juncture where you seek help from someone to unearth the answers for you or validate your hypothesis. If you are not able to find the solution, I am certain that you will be jittery with the need for a solution always at the back of your mind.

This is where powerful questioning comes to your aid. The most powerful questions cause people to search in a new direction – towards a new insight, action or commitment. They are delivered with timing and rapport, honoring the person and where they are at this point.

What makes a question a powerful one?

They are the ones that have a significant, positive impact on the quality and direction of a person current thought process on an issue that is important to them. Based on an analysis of hundreds of powerful questions and by observing how coaches and mentors use them, I have arrived at the characteristics of a powerful question:

1. Personal – it is about them, or about how they connect to an issue

2. Resonant – it has an emotional impact

3. Acute/ Incisive – it gets to the heart of the issue

4. Reverberating – it stimulates reflection both in the moment and afterwards

5. Innocent – the intent of the questioner is not self-interested or derived from an agenda of their own

6. Explicit – clearly and explicitly expressed

These characteristics make a convenient acronym – **PRAIRIE**. [Credits: David Clutterbuck, a Mentor & Coach]

Your first thought might be that this looks easy enough, but you would be wrong.

I myself have made the same mistake of arriving at a hasty conclusion. "Yes, I got it" is what I while running from my boss's cabin to write a report only to come back to him for 3-4 reviews before finalizing the document. The reason for this is that I am not evaluating the situation, nor am I asking about the purpose of the deliverables. I assume that I knew all the answers. I am partially correct, I know how to write a good report but without a 100% clarity on its purpose, mistakes are sure to creep in.

My boss said to me during a coffee break "when you say 'I got this' and have no concerns about a situation, that is when I get alarmed." What he meant was that as soon as I stop asking compelling questions, I assume that I know completely what's going to work and stop evaluating potential outcomes and solutions. It is a tendency all of us have when we want to take the short route. It's what holds us back from being a powerful leader.

Is powerful questioning an essential leadership habit?

It provides the leaders with a means to mitigate their confirmation biases and dive deep into the evaluation of a situation, a person or their team as a whole. Everyone has biases. The human brain is wired to jump to immediate conclusions, to look for shortcuts and how to procrastinate. (All natural qualities – I want my wife to read this line without fail)

Humans always love jumping to conclusions, filling gaps in stories (with their vivid imaginations) and tying up everything with a neat bow. According to neurologists, our brain rewards us with dopamine whenever we recognize and complete patterns, whenever we fill in the gaps and reach an understanding about something.

The problem is we don't have to be right to get this dopamine hit: we just need to think we're right. Certainty matters more than accuracy.

If you do not believe it then look at this video to test yourself. Is your brain wired as I have said?

URL: https://youtu.be/vKA4w2O61Xo

This brings us to the next step in our search:

How does a powerful question look like?

A powerful question (as stated above) should evoke clarity, create greater possibility, reveal new learning and generate action.

A powerful question …

Is open-ended: Ask what, when or how instead of asking a pointed yes or no.

Comes from a beginner's mindset: Start by telling yourself, "I don't know the answer."

Is clear and succinct: Keep it simple, don't use too many words.

Is impactful: It's important to remember that not every question in a conversation should be powerful. In a 30-minute conversation, aim for 2-3 powerful questions.

Happens in the moment: Here is probably the most crucial point to remember: You can't plan it! You have to be in the moment, all planned questions fall on their face every time.

You may be wondering how you could possibly remember all this. Well it is an easy answer – you need to be listening very carefully to what the other person is conveying. If you are connected to the content, it is very easy.

Let me take this opportunity to list a few questions as examples to make my point clearer:

Alternative:

• If you had a choice, what would you do?

• In what way do you think you can do it differently?

Appraisals:

• What do you make of it – the last years efforts?

• How do you feel about your contribution?

• How does the next year look to you?

Failures, preparation for

• What if it doesn't work the way you wish?

• And if it fails, what is your next action?

• What do you want it to be?

The next logical step: How do I master it?

What is curiosity? Find any 5-year old child and watch them for an hour. They will ask what, why and how to nearly everything new they see around them. They just want to know more and do not limit themselves to societal conventions of right or wrong. They just ask.

We are all born with this trait and our formal education trained us meticulously to lose it. As we grow older we start assuming outcomes and stop exploring. We at times do not want to make a fool of ourselves in a crowd by admitting 'I don't understand'. So we just keep quiet.

The secret to asking a powerful question is very simple: it is triggering our 5-year old selves and reconnecting with our curiosity.

Here is a small effort to rekindle your curiosity – "What has a head, a tail, is silver in colour and has no legs?"

In trying to figure this out, you have started looking at possibilities: What kind of animal has no legs? Is it an animal? What else could it be? What has a tail? Etcetera Etcetera.

It's the little kid inside of you wanting to understand, to know. Curiosity is the genuine desire to learn more and to explore.

Still haven't figured out the answer?

It's a 2 rupee coin.

Powerful questioning allows us to go deep and explore a lot of avenues which we may not have found on a superficial probe. Once we have clarity and the depth of knowledge, it will only help us get better. It will leave us in a much higher state of mind than when we started questioning.

So to sum it up – start kindling that curiosity to reach a clearer state of mind. Ask yourself if this author deserves praise for this chapter or not as the first exercise. I look forward to the results.

Now that we have got this into our system, the next thing we need to know is simple – what is that secret weapon that ensures success?

Based on the thoughts of many leaders who have done introspection and powerfully questioned themselves, it has been found that self-disruption is the one thing which will always keep you ahead in the race.

What is self-disruption? We all know that nothing but change is constant in the current business and corporate world. Some of the changes are drastic and some are incremental. Even if changes do not occur, a leader must every now and then change his approach to keep him ahead of the competitors.

This change is called disruption by the self.

Can you disrupted yourself by finishing the next chapter now?

Self-disruption is a secret weapon for success

"The only thing that is constant is change" - *Heraclitus*

We have all heard this often enough. However, our education system and society have never equipped us with the survival skills to accept change. Change has been a part of man's evolutionary journey since apes began walking on two legs.

What is meant by change?

The dictionary definition is to "make or become different" which is straightforward enough. But how should a leader view change? Markets may change, technology may change, the weather may change, and the business goals may change. There is not much that is fixed.

The only way to be risk-free is by by getting the basics right - supporting good habits, giving right feedback at the right time, suggesting good goals and developing a healthy network. We already know this, but when change happens we forget it. A clear and stable understanding of the system is what will keep us in equilibrium like Alice running furiously but staying in the same place in Through The Looking Glass. What it means is that winners or leaders need to embrace change in order to move forward.

In today's world, we are not only talking of change but also the speed of change. Hence anyone keeping up with the market needs to change, adapt or self-disrupt to stay ahead (or even stay in) the race.

What is disruption?

At the core of the business context, disruption can be defined as the act of creating a better value proposition in the same industry or creating a new market where there was none. The best example which comes to me immediately is Netflix (since my son is watching it currently even after my repeated orders to turn it off). Netflix was a disruptor to Blockbuster in the home video and DVD market.

Here is a crazy idea – what happens if innovation is mixed with disruption? You will have a Disruptive Innovation. Just like a startup, unless we disrupt ourselves, we get stuck in the same groove and forget to change – we forget to innovate ourselves and question the meaning of our life.

There is a Tamil saying "குண்டுசெட்டில குதிரை ஓட்டறது" which means to remain in the same place without any improvement. Neale Donald Walsch once said: "Life begins at the end of your comfort zone." Simply put, it means that you will move forward only when you let go of your fears and anxiety. Unfortunately, many of us have problems with leaving our comfort zones. We want to do more in life but are afraid to challenge ourselves and push the envelope on what we think is safe.

There are many among us who have no idea that they are caught in this space, or if they do, they don't know how to leave.

Here are 3 simple questions which we can ask ourselves:

- Check your energy levels. Are they low?
- Are you following patterns?
- Do you feel down?

If the answer to one or more of this question is YES then it is high time to self-disrupt.

You must put in the work to improve your current situation. It is driven by you and for you, so that you may serve others. My answer was a yes to questions 2 and 3 and that's why I went into self-disrupt mode.

So let's look at how you can self-disrupt:

Do something drastic in quick time

That's why in my self-disrupt quest, I did what I've never done before: I started a blogging site within 48-hours and aimed to have 50 blogs done in 90 days.

Kind of crazy, especially as I have never even typed a leave letter before in my life. I didn't give a damn about what people thought. I just wanted to enjoy the process.

Self-disruption requires rapid and immediate action. You need to make a decision that's going to teleport you a million miles away from your current reality, come up with a rapid plan and then enable it in less than 48 hours of notice.

911 – Should be reachable

"Houston we have a problem," said the captain and then the entire NASA team in earth was on board to help them (made famous by the movie Apollo-13). Similarly, you have to declare that you have a problem and are going to work on it. If you want to get into self-disrupt mode then you need to have your digital devices in FLIGHT MODE. This process will not work if social media and other distractions are reminding you of everything that has put you in this situation.

In your smartphone, the flight mode can only dial 911 and furnish your current location. What happens is that since you are going outside your comfort zone, there should be someone whom you can rely on helping you if you have any problems.

People will understand, or you can help them understand.

DIY

Avoid the temptation of bringing others in with you. Self-disruption as the term describes is very individualistic. There cannot be a partnership in this act. Self-disruption is a solo journey that needs only you. It's a selfish endeavor in a way, but it translates to helping others at the end of the process.

I did my recent self-disrupt process by myself. It was hard at first but I decided to bring a small and useful gift to my wife every day after returning from the office for 50 continuous days without a break. I could have outsourced the buying or could have bought some gifts in bulk but did not do so since I wanted to be my own physical effort. It was crucial that I returned home daily and made her even happier than the day before. I have never gifted her anything before without any reason, hence this disruption changed the whole way of how I looked at gift giving.

Some things in life must be done on your own. The decision that you need to disrupt yourself has to be made by you. You can't transfer the responsibility of these decisions to someone else.

Factor time for self-reflection daily

Make sure that you block sufficient time in your daily routine to do nothing. For your self-disrupt process, you'll need to contemplate every aspect of your life. This takes huge amounts of time - so schedule it in.

For me, Self-Reflection is the way to remove inner roadblocks, to first become aware of the things that are really holding me back and then tackle them by finding a solution.

Ask yourself a question about your life's work that is crazy.

Redesign your passion

Mine currently is writing (it used to be sleeping). Yours may be cooking, traveling, bird watching or trekking. It doesn't matter what it is. Do you still enjoy doing it? How does it make you feel? There is always a debate on whether your passion can change or is a constant.

In my view, I feel it is very subjective. People like me who have varied interests and skills do change their passion from time to time and there are many who have fixed on one. It is for you to find out where you fall and move forward.

Redefining your passion doesn't mean a complete makeover but making small adjustments within the current dimensions. In my case, it began as with writing blogs and now have I redefined it to trying to write a fiction novel. The base is writing and the redefinition is only in the output: from a BLOG to a MYSTERY BOOK.

Do that one thing which you are afraid of doing publically

Mine was drawing. I have done a bit of cartooning and then stopped it (frankly, my family asked me to stop after seeing a few of my creations). After that, a mental block formed that I cannot draw. As part of my self-disruption process, I have recommitted to trying my hand at cartooning.

I have made this promise to myself, and now to the whole world through this book. I have also got the physical copy of the book "Drawing on the right side of the brain".

There will be many such goals in your life which you can pick up and start – and you will definitely start to feel good about it.

Go back to the roots of who you were

In my case, it was to inspire others through the output of my self-development. In a way, over time I drifted slightly away from friendship and people. Then during the self-disruption process I have come back to forming connections with people connect and working closely with my group. Once you have captured that thread of your basic DNA, it is just a matter of adding new ingredients to take you to the next level.

The new ingredients can be got by doing the following

   • You must break the pattern.

- Question old philosophies.
- Do a clean out

Go out there and start disrupting yourself, go and innovate on yourself and you'll thank me for it one day.

Now that things have settled with disruption it should also be worth noting that disruption alone cannot bring you success. You need other traits as well - the next of which is flexibility. Most of us would be wondering if leaders can be flexible.

There is a generally accepted rule of thumb that leaders should be stern, clear, unflinching - and here I am saying that to be a leader you need to be flexible. Is there a mistake in one of the two statements?

No, both of them are true. Leaders need to be firm or flexible when the occasion calls for it. When should a leader be flexible?

- To trust in the team
- Increase loyalty
- Create an amicable environment
- Gives way to diversity
- Make connections/network
- Supports the infrastructure for SUCCESS.

So why don't you be flexible enough to turn to the next chapter before thinking of putting this book down?

Being Flexible is a MUST for success

Flexibility is a Must

The world is always in a state of flux. To thrive in this state, we need to evolve by thinking out of the box and being flexible enough to adapt to changing situations. But constant re-invention is not feasible or sustainable. So being flexible is your best bet. Keep in mind though that flexibility has its boundary as well - which in the business context is the company's core value system.

Sometimes your mind does not allow you to be flexible. The biggest mental barrier takes the form of biases or to put it more crudely - your EGO. Other mental obstacles include a lack of openness, too much pride, narrow vision and a lack of self-awareness.

Let's look at the issues that arise from the above. A proud or vain leader is focused on his own ideas and perceptions of reality. There will be no openness and loyalty in the team. Sometimes leaders get lazy and use the same "filter" or "lens" for every situation that comes along. This kind of narrow vision will eventually demotivate the team. A strong and individualistic leader is not a problem. The problem arises only when the leader is not aware of the impact of his behaviour on the team members and the work culture.

Let me take you through the lessons from my own journey.

Most of us begin our journey with an idea of what we want to do. We have a certain image of what the journey and its path will look like. We would have also done our due diligent research. We are all set. This excitement and adrenaline help our mind charge ahead with full-steam.

The bow is pulled back and we are ready to release our idea to the world. This was me a few months ago. All I saw was a straight trajectory to bulls eye. But then came one setback in my path after another.

My determination served as my fuel. It kept me going.

The adrenaline rush carried me through those times. But as truly stated in Indian folklore, this rush wanes without replenishment. The same happened to me too.

Discouragement, apathy, feelings of depression, doubts and other emotions crept in - sometimes all at once. I kept questioning myself - Could I pull myself out of these feelings? Was this all a fantasy that I may need to give up?

The trajectory was no longer straight. There were twists and turns, starts and stops, ups and downs. This is the pattern that now governs my life even today.

Decision time

It was decision time for me. Do I keep going? Do I abandon my dream? Was I delusional and crazy? Can I get through this phase? These were some of the questions I had to process on an hourly basis. There were no clear answers (which to be honest I still don't have), but something inside of compelled me to continue progressing towards my goal.

I realized that I had to be as flexible as I possibly could be. The twists and turns, zigs and zags, ups and downs, would have dealt a crippling blow had I remained inflexible.

I can draw parallels between this phase of my life reminded and Kambli and Tendulkar's innings against the West Indies. The Windies had bounced Kambli out while all Tendulkar did was to be flexible enough in bending and ducking those fiery bouncers. That series marked the end of Kambli's career. This made me realize that when we head towards obstacles head-on, sometimes it best to be flexible to come out safely without being smashed to pieces.

Most of the time it is better to be like an ant and move around the obstacle rather than move through it. When hindered by an obstacle ants stop, recalibrate their route and then continue. This is exactly what is meant by being flexible as a leader. Vinod Kambli could have extended his fabulous career if only he had learned to be humble. His compatriot Sachin who went on to have a legendary career for the next 20 years by doing just that.

As I hung on for my dear life, I realized that I needed to adjust to and accept changes as well. I made the necessary immediate changes so I could stay on the ride without being thrown off.

Adapting quickly

These changes came in the form of tweaking my initial idea, throwing out what was no longer relevant or that which no longer worked, and adding additional parts that made more sense at the new point in the journey. What was left after all the modifications was hardly recognizable as what I began with. Nonetheless, I was moving forward and it was much better. I felt re-energized and ready to go all the way.

I adopted a flexible mindset, which became my new norm. But here is a valid concern you may have. What happens if I cannot be a flexible person? How can I change my mindset and behaviour overnight? Not a problem at all. I have 4 steps that might work for you:

Step#1: Listen to your risk-averse inner voice

As you approach a challenge, this mindset will always throw a voice in your mind – "Are you capable of doing this task? Maybe you do not have the talent", "What if you fail? You'll be termed a failure". These are common for all us.

You may start a task and promptly hear the voices – "Look I told you it was risky, now you are in a mess". "It's not too late to escape with an excuse."

Just listen to these voices first.

Step#2: Consider that you have a better choice

How you handle these inner voices when you hit an obstacle or challenge or criticism is completely your choice. You can interpret them as a signal of weakness or lack of ability or talent. The other way is to try and see the same situation from the other side. It is as a signal to ramp up your abilities, stretch your efforts, expand your control and also take risks by abandoning the fear of failure.

Step#3: Talk back audaciously - with a positive mindset

As you approach a challenge here is what you will normally hear and how do you counter it. This short role play will make this point clearer:

Old mindset: "Are you sure you can do it? Maybe you do not have the right skills"

New mindset: "Yeah I'm not sure I can do it now but I think I can learn with time and effort"

Old mindset: "What if you fail – you'll termed a loser"

New mindset: "Most successful people have started with failure, and have had failures along the way before reaching their destination"

Old mindset: "Don't venture, it is better to back off now and be safe"

New mindset: "If I don't try I fail automatically, someone else takes the credit. Where is the dignity in that?"

Step#4: Choosing the positive mindset – and the actions

Over time, the course of action you take will define your journey whether you:

- Take on the challenge wholeheartedly

- Learn from your failures or setbacks and try again

- Take the criticism and act on it

The bottomline: Stay committed to your decision/goal but be flexible in your approach. Try to take a positive approach to every challenge that comes your way. If you feel the above 4 steps are a little difficult then let me give you another set of simple and easy tips.

Here are the 3 easy tips on how to adopt a flexible mindset:

1. Elaborate your available options

Quitting is certainly not an option. If that is how you are thinking, you need some serious introspection. At every juncture where you are unclear just ask yourself these 2 questions:

A) What are the alternatives available for me (list them all down no matter how crazy they are)

B) What change can I make that will be enough to move one step ahead from where you are currently?

2. Find your tribe

Find and associate yourself with those who have a similar wavelength or share a similar journey or vision.

Make sure that you find a group of people who are doing what you want to be doing. They should be a couple of steps ahead of you but not too far ahead. If they are too ahead, it will be more detrimental than helpful to you.

3. Reconfirm your 'why'

It is very important that you go back and remind yourself of why you are chasing this goal/dream. Remind yourself of how you felt–your frustration with life as it was. What you will find is that once you have explored these tips, your mindset will become more flexible.

"The measure of intelligence is in the ability to change." – *Albert Einstein*

How do you react when things do not go as expected? Do you take deep breaths, talk to a friend, or struggle? Do not collide with the obstacle, try to navigate around it.

Coming to the next question you may have - what is the best time of day to practice any of the new habits and tips you have learned from this book so far. Morning, evening, night or never?

The easy answer is to say that it depends on your lifestyle. Yet, there are some cultural habits which may say otherwise.

Indian culture by and large is driven by solar timing and it has always prescribed early morning as the best time for all productive work. This means waking up early is not an option but a necessity. Why not try it out if you don't believe in it.

Early Rising

Waking up early is possible

Time is a very funny concept. The easiest thing to do with time is waste it. Seldom can you find people who say they have copious time to do all their activities in. What comes to my mind on procrastination is Mark Twain's favourite quote: *"Never put off till tomorrow what may be done day after tomorrow just as well."*

Procrastination is not, as it may appear to be, a problem of time management. This habit is that is formed not created at birth. It actively looks for distractions shift focus from the task at hand. In a nutshell, many of us procrastinate to protect ourselves, our ego, from failures, from critical judgments, from making an extra effort to finish the task. Yet there are hints of "I can work better under pressure" or "I think I can finish this job before tomorrow sunrise".

Why am I talking about procrastination when the topic is something else? Just stick with me. Laziness, lethargy and procrastination are the major roadblocks for you to inculcate the habit of rising early in the morning. You must be wondering what you should bother waking up early at all. ?

Mornings are generally considered to be the best time to do your most productive work since the mind is fresh and agile. The environment is also very calm, with minimal distractions that are common during the rest of the day. When you wake up early you feel refreshed. You aren't thinking about too much yet or worrying about all the things you may need to do in the day. If you complete a short practice the first thing in morning, you are likely to succeed in that task on a regular basis.

A few months ago, I was watching a TV show on how to be more productive. One of the main points which came up was that you had to be a morning person. It was nice to hear and see, but to actually implement – my god it is mind blowing. Imagine cozy mornings and snoozing your alarm for ten minutes. and realizing that an hour has passed since when you finally wake up.

One evening, I was browsing through some CDs for some carnatic when I stumbled upon the திருப்பாவை (ML Vasanthakumari's Thiruppavai CD), the CD skipped to track 12 which said:

கனைத்திளம் கற்றெருமை ...
சினத்தினால் தென்இலங்கைக் கோமானைச் செற்ற
மனத்துக்கு இனியானைப் பாடவும்நீ வாய் திறவாய்
இனித்தான் எழுந்திராய் ஈதென்ன பேர்உறக்கம்!

அனைத்து இல்லத்தாரும் அறிந்தேலோர் எம்பாவாய்.
Translated:

kanaitthiLam kattrerumai ...
sinandhingu thennilangai kOmAnai chettra
manatthykku iniyAnai pAdavum nee vai thiravAi
initthAn ezundhirAi eedhenna pErurakkam
anaitthu illatthArum arindhElOrempAvai

The Meaning: You, the sister of the rich man in whose house the buffaloes give abundant milk... We have come here to your doorstep and stand with dew drops falling on our heads. Wake up, why is this long sleep? Come and sing of the Lord who wrathfully vanquished the lord of Lanka.

After watching the show, listening to the CD and then actually reading the meaning of the verse, I got excited and wanted to become a morning person myself, but the doubt persisted. I used to wake up early during my college days and then totally forgot about it soon after. I had been carrying over this New Year resolution year after year, but this year I wanted it to change.

As always I still doubted my ability to become a morning person?

First of all, yes. It is possible. It is not as far-fetched as trying to become a professional basketball player if you are only 5'2". This is more like trying to change a belief system and a set of habits which you have grown comfortable with. You can do it if you are dedicated and intentional.

The one most significant enemy to acquiring this habit is our own mind. There is always a voice which tells us that to get up early we may need to sleep early and by doing that we may lose some of the best times of the day. We postpone what we want to do and what we know will give us satisfaction in the long-run because it feels too threatening at the moment.

Let's assume that you have overcome the anxiety and are now ready to take the test. The next hurdle? Answering yourself when you ask "why should I lose my beauty sleep to worry about what I can achieve by getting up early? "

To address this question I researched some studies on sleep patterns, and these are the benefits they showcased

Make more money

The first thoughts in our minds when we wake up are about money and work. This puts the entire day in focus and helps you to do a lot more than waking up late with hazy thoughts and sleepy eyes.

Be more productive

Not only does it allow more time for both productivity and leisure, it also makes our days less stressful. It gives us that much more time to relax and pace ourselves rather than constantly trying to 'catch-up'.

Be healthier

Early risers generally have better sleep patterns than night owls. Additionally, growth hormones are released that are essential for muscle development after a good night sleep.

Be more happy and satisfied

You might still be tired from your day's work, but mentally you can unwind surrounded by those you love in a relaxed setting.

Another perk of being an early rise is some uninterrupted quiet time with your significant other.

So can you go from being a sleepyhead to a morning bird? Here are 9-steps that will get you going:

1. Change the story line

We have heard so many people say "I am not a morning person, I prefer late nights". Do you think there is any biological evidence for it? When we study them we find that it is just perception and preferences built over the years. So try changing the story line from today and begin telling yourself "I am a morning person". [Note: Psychology tells us that we always adjust our behaviour to fit our stories]

Before attempting to set the alarm or go and purchase a non-snoozing alarm, try to get into the right mindset first. Once you have internal approval, make the move towards implementation. The best way to internalize this is by changing the story line from "I CAN'T" to "I CAN".

2. Find what's in it for you

Whenever you want to achieve some goal or change a behaviour pattern, you need to start articulating the importance of that change. You need to take a notebook and start writing what would happen to you if you became a morning person, then right down what is the risk if you don't become one. Stare at this paper till the actual value of the change emerges in your brain. Once you get it, it will motivate you even after the initial enthusiasm wares off.

3. Fixed sleep time

To change the pattern you need to end up making changes in your sleep timings. You cannot probably sleep at the same time as you do today and then try getting up early tomorrow. Your body will resist since it has been made to get used to certain hours of sleep over the years. So if you fix your waking hours at 5:30am and then work backwards to plan your sleep timing and follow that pattern. You should ideally give yourself around 6.5 hours of sleep time.

4. Use an alarm device

Since I have now been trained to get up early in the morning I feel no need for the alarm but in the initial phase it was my only saviour. Whether you use an alarm clock (like me, an old timer), a smart phone or a fitness tracker, place your alarm beyond your arm's reach - to make sure you need to get up physically to shut it off, by which time you are awake.

5. Complete Lights Out

The environment provides subtle cues to your body, so it can learn the right response. When it gets dark, your body naturally begins preparing itself for sleep (unless you have conditioned it otherwise). When it gets bright, you naturally begin waking up. Use this to your advantage.

6. Choose your outfits before you sleep

Usually when you get up, you are not in a good position to decide. It is better to be dressed for what you want to first as soon as you wake up, that makes you less likely to change your clothes and go back to sleep. If you plan to exercise, then get your track pants on the night before itself. Yes, initially you may sleep with the track pants on but do not deter from this tip – it's very important.

7. Drink some liquid

The first thing after getting up is to have a beverage, preferably a hot one. Since I do not drink coffee, it's not on my menu but I drink hot water with lime and honey. Have any drink you prefer (except for one with spirit, you need spirit only in your heart)

8. Have a bad cop near you

You need to find a mentor or a person who can police you and hold you accountable. Explain to the person why you need to make this change and why it is important that you stick to this routine. Move on to the next step only after you have found that someone.

9. Commit to 41 days

The western rule says 21 days but I would like to stick with our traditional method of one Mandalam (41 days). The background behind the mandalam concept is the number of days between 2 full moon (30 days) and the number of days to the next Ekadashi (11 days), totaling to 41. If you can do this for 41 days, you can do this for longer.

Let me not lie. The underlying motive behind this chapter is not to make you get up early. It is just to convey the message that you have more power inside you than you think you know. You don't have to rue and be hard on yourself. You have all the powers to change your habits and preferences so that you can go and achieve all your dreams. Go and aim for the moon (and don't forget to send me a selfie when you get there).

During my summer holidays when I used to be young (quiet a long time back) I used to go to Manargudi, a place near Kumbakonam. Most of my vacation time was spent in that village and the only past time there was to go to our ancestral property and watch the farming and gardening process in the morning. It was a nice activity to do – everyone would be farming and I just used to sit in the easy-chair and watch them.

Little then did I know that there were many a common things between farmers and leaders. Does it sound a bit weird?

What is the connection between a Farmer & a Leader?

Farmers and leaders - the connection

Come summer time in my younger days, we were always sent to our grandparent's house for vacations. For many years in continuity I have traveled to மன்னார்குடி (Mannargudi) [Note: no way am I related to the infamous family]. The only pastime would be to go and play in the open fields where farmers grew tomatoes, rice, sugar cane and bananas.

The daily life of a rural Indian farmer, from my limited experience, is that they would start the day by milking their cows. Once finished they would get his lunch packed and head straight to the fields to do one of the following: irrigation, ploughing, weeding and any others operations in the field. In the afternoon, they have lunch , rest under the tree and then finish the remaining work before sunset – come back home, have dinner and rest. They are the ones who get the best sleep possible.

They haven't any interest in gold or silver or any types of cosmetics. They grow the real gold which are the crops. Like parents they watch over the crops day and night. They become the guardians of the crops from the stray cattle. What this means is that they lead the simplest life in India. I assume that they love living very close to nature but I haven't verified my assumption.

Coming back to the present, my vacations are to book reservations in resorts, beach getaways, farm stay and the word "farmers" has been cut out completely from my vocabulary. Even the highways do not have much greenery for my kids to enjoy what I did in the 80s while traveling. Are we really going away from nature in trying to chase something that does not bring us any joy?

So to learn more about farming (which I do not know much about even after learning) I reached out to one of my old friend's father who is still a practicing farmer and got to learn many tips about farming which needs to be extended to the leadership fraternity to make them a better leader. He was very happy that a big software professional was coming to him and asking for data. This really created a big smile on his face before he started.

Within a few minutes I was flabbergasted. There was so much to farming that we never even know how it is done. There was shifting agriculture, dry irrigation, drip irrigation, crop rotation, and sedentary cultivation and much more, many of them slipped out of my mind.

None of the school syllabuses ever care to teach our children how agriculture is done, but they are exposed to how BMW cars are made or how to use the iPhone. A pity state of affairs but let me come back to the moot point of the chapter.

So let's get to business.

Do you know the value of preparation?

I approached my friend's father and asked him what was needed to get a good yield of tomatoes for example. He took me out to his farm and we went into a mini-shed where he had created a greenhouse like condition. There were many boxes with dried seeds waiting to be planted. He said that he needed to create this greenhouse condition to increase the probability of a fruitful (pun unintended) harvest.

He touched upon the effects of greenhouse and its gases without having studied any science. He was also equipped to predict rain within a day's tolerance only by looking at the night sky and few animals that are in their surroundings. He told me that if cows lie down in the night, chances of rain are bright. The frogs always croak, but when the male frogs starts to do the mating-call croak then rain is in the air since frogs always lay their eggs in fresh water and they need to mate before the rain comes.

Back to our tomato plants story, pretty soon, after a few weeks, he would be scooping these boxes into a larger tractor and go to the field. There he would plow the field and have it leveled and ready for sowing. Then he would make sure that there were proper nutrients in the soil for growing tomatoes. He would have to exert a lot of human effort to plant these saplings into the field.

The plant have to be planted deep enough yet not too deep. It has to be watered yet not over watered. The roots had to be covered just enough to withstand wind and rain. These were conditions very similar to operating a nuclear fuel or an unstable compound. For example, tomato plant can only withstand temperatures between 21 - 26 deg Celsius and rainfall needs to be between low and medium.

Then he needs to tend to the plants such that weeds don't overtake the plants' growth. He would have to keep an eye out for the pest and diseases too. After 4-5 months he could take a bumper harvest of ripened tomatoes.

As a leader what do you see?

Whether it is farming or growing or leadership, the message is the same. It is loud and clear. Your job as a leader is to tend to something for a period of time so that you can harvest a potential fruit.

As a leader, how are you going to create a mini-greenhouse environment? How are you going to plow the field and make it ready for sowing? How to keep pests and diseases away? When are you going to harvest the fruits? These were the thoughts that came to me when he finished his explanation.

It would really be a waste of time as a leader if we choose to just throw the seeds and let nature take care of growing it. Are you thinking of natural progression of growth process for your team or do you want to GROW them?

Here are some points that are worth pondering:

1. Do you know where each team member is in the development process?

Plants require different types of handling based on their seedling, water requirements, and temperature and incubation period before they are ready for harvesting. When a plant requires so many handling types, then complex social animals like humans require much more individual attention to groom them. As leaders, we need to spend a lot of time initially in looking after the developmental needs of the team members.

2. Are your team's developmental plans done with one-size-fit-all?

The development plan for tomatoes is vastly different from ladies finger or water melon. Handling them with the same plan is a sure recipe for disaster. Each plant requires different amount of heat, water and irrigation methods and like-wise the learning ability of the team is never the same. We need to plan separately for each member or else the leader always fails.

3. Have you looked into the terrain to make sure the team does not fall or fail?

The furrows dug for each plant needs to be different and the water intake needs to be different. A well-organized team have a lot of variety within themselves. Some are night-howlers while some are early birds. Some work in isolation with complete focus while others may tolerate noise and disturbance to a level. So it's the leader's responsibility to create that field for each of the members to succeed.

You have not become a leader because you have the skill and knowledge. You were made as a leader so that you do not stand as a team with just one tall tree but as a forest. You as a leader have to nurture the team and grow them along with you. You need to sow, plough, irrigate, harvest. Just by sitting in the cabin with the title leader does not entitle you to the success that comes from doing all the above actions.

By the way, the farmers done with the harvest for one season are always ready for the next season with a different batch of plants. As a people leader, are you ready for the same?

Leadership is sometimes a thankless job.

A leader has a moral obligation to help all those who work for the common goal to succeed, be it their own direct reports, cross-functional team members, suppliers, vendors or customers. That is the primary purpose of a leader. To create an environment for them to succeed and when that moment comes – you need to step aside and let them savor the moment (remembering MS Dhoni after the world cup victory). It takes a lot of work, lot of effort and most of the time it is thankless.

If you see any of the above questions as tiring or not interesting to you, then leadership is not meant for you. Just try to ponder on these questions before venturing into this role.

Now that you know leadership is a thankless job, I'm about to tell you that everyone is a leader. Or in other words leadership traits have always been there within yourself. It is just that some of them have found it and used it to their advantage while others are still looking for it or not aware that it is inside them.

Let me quote a sloka from the Bhagvat Gita – Chapter 18, Sloka#43

शौर्यं तेजो धृतिर्दाक्ष्यं युद्धे चाप्यपलायनम् |
दानमीश्वरभावश्च क्षात्रं कर्म स्वभावजम् || 43||
**śhauryam tejo dhritir dākshyam yuddhe chāpy apalāyanam
dānam īśhvara-bhāvaśh cha kshātram karma svabhāva-jam**

<u>**Translation**</u>: Valour, invincibility, steadiness, skillful, resolve to never retreat from battle, generous, and leadership abilities, these are the natural qualities of work for Kshatriyas.

Here 'valour' means the ability to plunge into a battle without fear. 'Invincibility' is the capacity of the mind to remain undefeated by others. 'Steadiness' is the talent to complete a work that has been started with obstacles. 'Skillful' is the ability in executing the work with precision. 'Resolve to never retreat from battle' is not to flee a battle even when you are convinced of one's death. 'Generous' means parting of one's own possession to others even if they are your enemy. 'Leadership ability' means to govern all the above. These are the duties of a Kshatriya born in his inherent nature.

Kshatriya here can also apply to Administrators, Bureaucrats, Politicians, Businessmen, Presidents, PMs, CMs and so on!

Please note…

These qualities come naturally to a person who has perceived the answer to the question "Who am I"? He need not cultivate them, it's already there inside him.

Could not think of a better topic for the next chapter. Quite a fitting one to have looked at the required skills for a leader and then say it's all been there inside of you. This means that the only thing which you need to do is to look inwards to find the leadership skill. It's never an outbound training; it is always in-bound.

Curious to know how all that is required is inside of you all the while? Yes, then turn to the next chapter and If you will do that, my book will have achieved its purpose and you will be successful.

Its inside of you

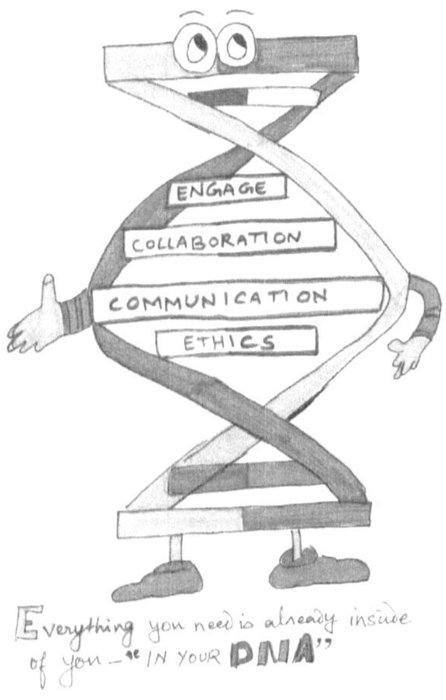

Everything you need is already inside of you – it's IN YOUR DNA"

It's inside of you

Who is a leader?

Why don't many of us believe we are leadership material?

These 2 questions come to my mind immediately when I look for the leadership DNA in everyone. These are interesting questions –because for me everyone is a leader and anyone who wants to make a difference ends up impacting someone somewhere, thereby becoming is a leader.

We all surely make a minimal impact to someone somewhere – so technically we are all leaders, many of us just don't believe in ourselves or our abilities. There are many preconceived notions of who a leader is and what abilities a leader must possess. Leadership doesn't mean acquiring power or trying to change the world. It can be as simple as activities in our day-to-day routine -helping a neighbor, listening to a friend, or standing up for a principle that we believe in.

Another gripe I have is that everytime I talk about a leader, folks always bring up examples of Steve Jobs, Bill Gates, the US Presidents, Hitler or Churchill etc. They don't have the ability to recognize the leaders amongst them first. Let's take the example of the devastating floods of 2015 that ravaged greater Madras (or now Chennai) and look at the leaders who emerged there. It was only the local residents and the younger generation who took charge of the situation and restored normalcy inch by inch. The holds true for the stoic fishermen tribe who shouldered the burden of the Kerala floods. Yet for some reason, we do not see these extraordinary acts as leadership skills. Even the ability to identify another leader amongst ourselves is in itself a leadership skill - one that most of us and have hidden within us.

So the difference according to me between a leader and not being a leader is that belief in the self. There are generally 4 ways to stake claim for this:

1. Believe that you have something to offer: It always starts with you and how you see yourself. What this means is the recognition that you have something to offer and create a positive impact on someone.

2. Dedicate yourself to make a change: You don't have to change yourself. You can make a difference by showing your compassion and good attitude – speak kind words, volunteer for social causes, support something which you strongly feel or any such meaningful thing.

3.Be sensitive to issues impacting others: Everyone will have some amount of sympathy and empathy. What I want to make you recognize is that you need to tap that natural DNA of empathy DNA. Don't listen at a superficial level – start going deep and try to understand the emotions, fears and hopes of the person you are listening to.

4. Making the first move: At the end of the day – only actions will speak and produce results. Successful leaders have the courage to take action while others hesitate. Don't just notice, don't just discuss: get up and do something.

If you find yourself resonating with any of the points mentioned above, you are ready to claim the mantle of a leader. Many people believe that leadership comes only with a formal role or position. But as a leadership & executive coach, I can tell you that isn't true - we are ALL leaders.

Robert Murray agrees with me and believes that everything you need to be a great leader is already inside you. "It's in your DNA."

Who is Robert Murray? He is the author of the famous book "It's Already Inside" (Kindle Version) which is a collection of well-told personal stories with solid leadership lessons.

I have to agree with the author when he says that many people graduating from our schools today do not have the ability to think critically. "Problem finders are everywhere," writes Murray. "Innovative problem solvers are rare. Imagination and thinking outside the box are scarce."

I have tried to hand-pick a few lessons which I felt are necessary to prove that Leadership skills are lying there inside you all waiting to be woken up from the deep slumber. I would like to echo my quotes from the Bhagvat Gita earlier with thoughts from Murray's western concepts.

Never Ignore The Corporate Grapevine

It comes in all forms. From brand violations to messy office space, from inconsistent customer service to poor employment practices and procedures, and to leadership apathy. It's your job as a leader to do everything within your power to ensure graffiti is removed immediately when it appears. It's easy to blame the system or wait for someone else to bell the cat but everyone would like to be in a safe position.

Imagine if you kept quiet when any of these events happened in your home - the person (children) responsible would get a good telling off. So why treat corporate any different? If you have the will to make amends of things in your home like being the bad cop for your child, the devil's advocate with your spouse, the front runner to help old age grandparents then why stop those traits only in your home? You can let loose of the same tendencies at your workplace. It makes you a better person and gets to change the system too.

Leadership Augmented Cockpit

You can fake or pretend your way through every scenario you come across. Yes sometimes it might work for some people but you can never rely on it for long term success. It will always seem like but when you look back from the finish line, you will find that they would not have crossed more than 75% of your destination.

You need to develop some form of Leadership Simulator that you can immerse yourself to design the best-case solutions for the complex problems. There is no one single solution to the problem. Since leadership styles vary and the situations that each leader undergoes is also different, it's very difficult to copy from one successful leader and implement it into for your situation.

So this simulator (or the exercise of building one) will enable you to think and respond quickly to unknown problems and keeps your stress levels under control. You need a testing ground and for most of us – home and family are the best groundsmen that we can get.

Pulse from Ground Zero

Survey each person in your business, from the janitor and those in the mail room to the accountant to the HR person. Ask them how their individual roles serve the customer, ask for their ideas to better serve the customer. Getting information from the streets or the driver network is the best information that you can have. If they are clueless, meet with the employee individually to explain his or her role as salesperson [NOT as a leader] for the company.

Those on the ground usually have the actual data or to be more accurate the precise information on the bottlenecks, roadblocks and risks. When sitting on top, it is very difficult to view all the nitty-gritty for smooth operations.

Just like how your wife would not be in a position to know the exact contents inside your fridge or the amount of biscuits left in the closet or the washing powder for the machine. Even though you are the head – it's quite impossible for you to collect all the data only by yourself. You need a helping hand at all levels.

Windows and Mirrors

Your stock as a leader (and leadership stock is measured by how much people trust you and will follow you on a journey) goes up significantly when you practice two simple "leadership optics" habits. Look out the window when times are good and look in the mirror when things aren't going so well.

Let's draw a parallel at your home – if you are very happy at home and had some good moments then you will immediately go and get some sweets or enjoy a weekend stay at some resort. All that you will think of is only the happiness and would like to explore more in that direction. Now if you have some unfortunate situations or bad financials or raptured relationship then the first thing that you do is to look for the root cause and see what you can do to come out of it. In short – you'll try to introspect yourself. If this is already inside of you, why not do the same in your corporate world?

Don't misunderstand the priorities of your Home

Home is NOT the place to go and vent about everything that frustrates you in your external job. Home is NOT the place you go to continue working like a dog, doing email and reports. Home, or your personal life, is the reason you go to work, because it is work that finances your personal life.

Home will be there much after you quit the job. The job is just a means to make the ends of your personal dreams and not the other way around. Understanding this valuable truth is not being disloyal to your organization or your entrepreneurial dreams; it is what will keep you balanced, healthy, and strong to be better at what you do!

These points are a quick summary of what resonated with me deeply and are sure to help you too. There are many other real-life examples on how to tap the skill to leverage your practices at home and apply them to succeed as a leader in the workplace The common mantra which I feel that everyone needs to utter is "leadership skills is inside of me and not outside". So, look for it inside and use it wisely to your gains.

Some of the questions that came up in my introspection with myself is listed below:

- The difference between a manager and a leader

- How to focus on the solution, not the problem

- How to stop wasting time in meetings

- When to overreact and when to under-react

- When to look stupid and when to act smart

- What looks will suit your style of leadership

And much more. So I urge you to go and find that leader within yourself and start your journey towards the ultimate dream.

I would like to quote a real-life example from my own role model and try to draw parallels between sports and leadership. I love cricket and loved it until I got married (there is no correlation between the two, this is just an innocent statement). But my admiration and respect for Rahul Dravid still remains – for the way he conducts himself both on and off the field.

He is a modern day Arjuna, whose focus is fixed only on to the eye of the bird that his master Drona tasked him to aim for. His skill, focus and attitude towards his game are unparalleled till today. I want to explore what I learned from this great gentleman who graced the cricket field along with the GOD of cricket Sachin.

Excited to move to the next page?

Rahul Dravid's Lessons

There are lots of leadership lessons that you can learn from "The Ramayana". Yes, I know this is a controversial topic, especially as the April 2019 assembly elections are around the corner as I write this. But I believe that this great Indian epic makes some interesting observations on leadership.

At 24,000 verses, the Ramayana is less hefty that the Mahabharata. It is still longer than both Homer's Greek epics the Iliad and the Odyssey combined! The story of the Ramayana is quite unlike the Mahabharata's story. The Mahabharata is a game of thrones-esque battle between two factions of a family. The Ramayana is a single man's quest to rescue his wife Sita after she is kidnapped by the demon king Ravana.

In his epic, story displays traits which are present only in a true leader. For example, he maintains composure in the face of the calamity that has befallen him (the kidnapping of his beloved wife). He sets about planning a search and rescue with his wife's safety and not revenge as an objective through his mission, he travels the subcontinent on foot and strikes up lasting friendships with those he meets on the way.

Rama does not hesitate in admitting Ravana's prowess as a warrior nor his character as a human - barring his obvious flaws. Rama also expresses how there is no need to condemn a person for certain qualities and instead condemn the qualities and work towards changing them. Another admirable quality of Rama is his ability to go through even the most extreme situations with grace and dignity.

Going from the world of epics to the grounds of cricket, let us explore the traits of Rahul Dravid's leadership. .

THE WALL as we all know him is a professional with high integrity and a well-defined set of habits. Former South African paceman Allan Donald recounted an incident with the then caption Dravid during a match in 1997. The 90s were famous (or infamous) for the culture of heated sledging during games. After one such display by Donald during the final of a triangular series, Donald felt contrite for his behaviour towards Dravid. However, Dravid, who was known for his grit, discipline and humble nature was so hurt by the incident that he didn't speak to Donald when the paceman approached him after the match.

Many do not know that he was the top scorer in the 7th ODI World Cup held in England. He finished with 461 runs, a perfect response to people who kept insisting that he was only a TEST batsmen and never good for the One Days.

In June '05 when I was in Bangalore completing some work at a gas agency where I saw two people emerge from a Santro (note the choice of car) - Mr. and Mrs. Dravid. With absolute no airs or pretense, they had come to fulfill all the requirements for a new gas connection like the aam aadmi, despite the owner's please to have his boy complete all the work from the comfort of their home. Dravid even obliged his adoring fans with pictures and autographs. Respect!

There are a lot of things which we can learn from his personal and professional life. As a salute to the great player, I thought I would list down the the top 7 leadership qualities which are very much associated with him.

1.

Substance Over Style– "The Big Fundamental" - Looking great is great, performing great is even better. Rahul did not win awards for style or flair. He did not have the aura of Sachin, the flamboyance of VVS or the artistry of Ganguly and yet was the match winner for India. Leaders must choose Substance over Style which Rahul displayed throughout his career.

2.

Greatness Is Appreciated More When it's Gone- His role in Indian cricket was never appreciated until he hung up his boots. The WALL certainly kept woes at bay and stood strong until till he retired - similarly a good leader should be felt by his absence rather than his presence.

3.

Quietly Be The Best At What You Do- Dravid was not outwardly expressive. He never showed any signs of aggression or panic or even jubilation - and just quietly went about doing what he knows best.

Leaders should also concentrate on doing what they know silently and ignore the negative environment around them.

4.

You Can't Care What People Think - Rahul was not a media darling, a cover star or sought after for endorsement, he just raked up the runs and played the big innings. He did not have a care for what was being spoken (or not) about his personality (or lack thereof) - his focus was only on winning matches.

5.

Nice Guys Don't Finish Last - Nice guys finish wherever they want to, and Rahul is the perfect example for this. After India was knocked out by Bangladesh in the World Cup in 2007, Dravid was graceful in accepting the defeat. He gifted two of his bats to the heroes of that match Tamim Iqbal and Mushfiqur Rahim. A gesture fitting of a true leader.

6.

Get Better With Age- Just like fine French wine, great leaders get better, lead better, make better judgment with age. The way Rahul matured as a charismatic leader is proof. His 2-day long innings with VVS (Eden Gardens 2001, Adelaide 2003) and his last test series in England (103*,117, 146*) define his maturity.

7.

Make Those Around You Better - Rahul consistently made his teammates, coach, country and the world of cricket better. He always served as the finest ambassador for the game. He changed the dynamics of the team unit with his presence. Leaders must also try to coach and mentor the teams - a proven formula for guaranteed success.

Rahul has exemplified how a leader has to be humble yet firm, goal oriented yet not lacking in social sensitivity, hardworking yet family oriented. Being aware of these traits may, you might wonder or worry about how you can acquire them. Dispel your doubts and urge to answer to others.

When the question of "So what am I trying to prove?" arises, it indicates self-doubt. Do not fall into this trap.

What are you trying to prove?

What is there to prove?

Certain records need to be set straight right here – leadership is about expressing and not proving. The moment one falls into the trap of 'proving', they start to lose a few important traits that make a leader. Leadership is all about being; and then doing. Everything a leader does reflects what he or she is. Therefore, leadership is about expressing oneself, not proving oneself (Quote from Warren G. Bennis)

I attend the December Marzhagi function every year without fail. It is the only month where you feel that Madras (or to be more precise

Music Academy, NaradaGana Sabha & Parthasarathy Swami Sabha) is heaven on earth. I have listened to 100s of Katcheris (or concerts) but classical music duo the RaGa sisters set a new precedent this time before their concert commenced - something that changed the perspective of what came next. They began by wishing the audience a Happy New year and added "thank you for letting us serve you with our divine music".

This statement is not a new one, nor is it free of cliches, what followed it was the exciting part. The sisters began by unleashing their repertoire in a raw, unadulterated form. The accompanying artists (on the violin and the mridangam) followed suit. The artists then were in unison, expressing their emotions and allowing the audience bask in the brilliance of their real-time extempore.

The audience connect that this concert established was far greater than that with the classical rendition of the songs. The artists stopped trying to prove their ability, their strength and their intellectual proviso and only were interested in bringing out the pure emotions of the song. All they did was to express the bare emotions (bhava) of the song – nothing pathbreaking, but it made all the difference .

Similarly, a leader must also reveal their true self in front of the team. We often desire to 'act' like a leader than being driven from the inside by the need to lead.

What is the difference between this desire and drive?

When you act out of desire you are trying to prove something to someone whereas when it is a drive from the inside, you are trying to express yourself.

Growing up, you will be faced with many challenges and perhaps the biggest of them is (notwithstanding finding a spouse) to overcome the self-doubt about your abilities. The bad news is that there is no way to avoid this feeling. The good news is that it happens to all.

In seeking the answer as to why do our brains have created a compulsion to 'prove', here are some templates of the thoughts we have:

"X" is better than me because…

I'm having "X" years of experience and yet I have not achieved anything

Maybe I am too weak; I can't deal with this pressurized environment

I have wasted my time by making this huge mistake

They expect me to be "X" but I can't which means …

I have had all these forms of self-doubt until I finally found a way to break this chain. Let me tell you how I did it.

Have you ever run into an old acquaintance from your past -someone detested and always felt the need to prove your worth around? Maybe the last time you saw each other was in school and all of you have moved on to a high-flying career. Or maybe you're experiencing a new low in your work and just feel the need to impress someone (and vicariously yourself). There would have been some circumstance or the other at some point in our life where we felt the need to prove ourselves to someone. I want to share my own story of a recent encounter that left me feeling anxious to prove myself.

One weekend when I was in a cafe enjoying a cup of evening Tea with my wife, I ran into a group of acquaintances who were my nemesis at my previous job. They knew me when I was at a different stage of life and probably still thought of me as the immature, insecure me who was still trying to prove my importance.

As we bumped into each other (unfortunately), I listened as they boasted about their achievements since we last met. When one of them asked what I had been up to, I immediately felt an impulsive desire to prove to this group that I had grown more successful than them since we last met. I didn't like that sudden, defensive feeling, so I paused, sipped my tea and then quietly shared some general updates about my family and moved on." [Signs of maturity - Yes]

What I realized after being in a leadership role for a while is that the moment you start feeling the need to impress someone is the moment you need to walk away. Just get yourself out of that place. Doing this with grace and dignity will enhance your image more than anything else can. At some point or another you have to accept that if you are spending your life trying to prove yourself to others, it is probably your own approval you are lacking.

So here are the question you have to let your gut answer:

- Where does the instinctive desire to prove ourselves come from?
- Why is it so important to let others know how important we are?

Self-Preservation

Those of you who have studied personality wiring can probably pinpoint a few triggers deep within our personality types that cause this knee-jerk reaction to validate ourselves. For me, I realized where some of my natural insecurities came from the results of an ENFP (Extraversion iNtuitive Feeling Perception) test. That is how I was able to nail the culprit. You can take a short online ENPF test to find out more about your own personality type and its associated strengths and drawbacks. Consequently, I had to confront the defensive pride which I had built up to ensure that it would not prompt actions or words I would later regret.

Now, what about you? What are you trying to prove? What is the insecurity in your life that is governing and limiting your positive influence on others?

In the book *"Making Your Leadership Come Alive"* by **Jeremie Kubicek,** he writes about the plague of self-preservation. The moot point is that when you overprotect what you are afraid of losing, you will lose it sooner. Trying to prove yourself actually ends up hurting you more because when fear begins to take over, your actions always fail you.

These actions that you perform to prove your worth end up undermining your credibility in the eyes of others. It leads to bragging or exaggeration, ultimately resulting in you being perceived as a self-important or arrogant person. Once built, these perceptions take a lot to change and hence need to handle with utmost care.

A simple exercise I found using Google helped me understand the concept of a complete leader. When I typed "Leader with something to prove" into the search bar, results in the first page all related to sports - which gave me the clear indication that when a leader tries to prove something there is always a winner and a loser. When I fine-tuned the search criteria to "a leader with something to express" the results were more inclined towards how a person could become better, exceptional, focused professional leaders.

Nothing to Prove, Nothing to Hide, Nothing Lose!

It is imperative to become fluent in self-awareness so that one can regulate and lead themselves when self-preservation guides their behavior. If we can state these phrases honestly and accurately in our lives, we will become leaders worth following:

I have nothing to Prove!

I have nothing to Lose!

I have nothing to Hide!

How far away are you from being at this stage of secure, confident humility?

Life is an ongoing journey of self-awareness, but if you approach each day with a drive to regulate your patterns to avoid insecurities controlling you, then you gain an increasingly greater ability to focus on others more than yourself.

What else is there to prove if we can focus on others?

Your whole life is an ongoing journey of self-awareness, but if you approach each day with a drive to regulate your patterns so that your insecurities can't control you, you will gain an increasingly greater ability to focus on others more than yourselves.

What else is there to prove if we can focus on others?

As leaders, are others being drawn into your artistic expression or are they being distracted by your drive to prove your own worth? This is a very important question which I would like you to ponder about before we proceed.

We have come to the conclusion of the first part of my book where I have tried to explore and discover many hidden facets of the traits of leadership. I like you to pause here and try to implement a few of the tips you have read so far to really understand yourself and get to know your strengths and possible weaknesses to work on .

Discovery is a great process and is a required one for a leader from time to time. Each person has a unique temperament and relationship with fear, love, creativity and focus. Hence I urge you to choose your vehicle to self-awareness based on what suits you the most but also leverage the tips explained in this book to enjoy the fruits of your pursuit.

"செறிவறிந்து சீர்மை பயக்கும் அறிவறிந்து ஆற்றின் அடங்கப் பெறின்." - திருக்குறள் Verse 123

Transliteration: "seRivaRindhu seermai payakkum aRivaRindhu aatrin adangap peRin" – Thirukkural Verse 123

<u>**Meaning:**</u> Knowing that self-control is knowledge, if a man should control himself, in the prescribed course, such self-control will bring him distinction among the wise. In other words, comprehending and acquiring self-control confers upon one the esteem of wise men.

Self-control comes only from self-awareness. I truly wish all of you discover your true self and thereby find success in your future endeavors.

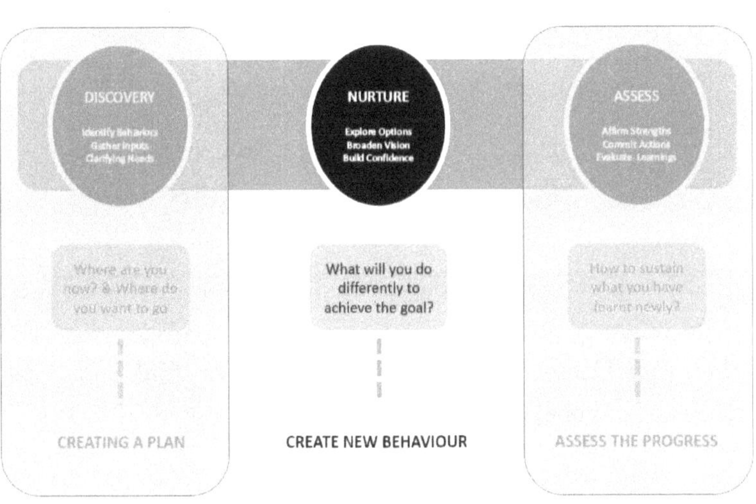

DISCOVERY
Identify Behaviour
Gather Inputs
Clarifying Needs
NURTURE
Explore Options
Broaden Vision
Build Confidence
ASSESS
Affirm Strengths
Commit Actions
Evaluate Learnings
Where are you now? & Where do you want to go
What will you do differently to achieve the goal?
How to sustain what you have learnt newly?
CREATING A PLAN
CREATE NEW BEHAVIOUR
ASSESS THE PROGRESS

Igniting Inspiration

"When your Daemon is in charge, do not try to think consciously. Drift, wait, and obey." — *Rudyard Kipling*

Qualities of Inspiration

In a success and money-obsessed corporate structure and a blind, factory-like education system, the skill of 'inspiration' is often overlooked. Inspiration awakens us to new possibilities by allowing us to transcend our ordinary experiences and limitations. Inspiration may sometimes be overlooked because of its elusive nature. Its history of being treated as supernatural or divine hasn't helped us at all.

Inspiration has 3 main qualities according to many psychologists;

evocation, transcendence, and approach motivation. First, inspiration is evoked spontaneously without intention. Secondly, Inspiration also transcends our more animalistic limitation to reveal a moment of clarity and awareness of new possibilities. Finally, inspiration involves approach motivation, in which the individual strives to transmit, express, or actualize a new idea or vision. [Taken from Psychologists Todd M. Thrash & Andrew J. Elliot research material]

A study by McKinsey & Company on leadership found that inspirational leadership is the best way to help organizations make significant (and efficient) change and improvement. It is the most powerful way to lead as it creates more energy, excitement and commitment in people than any other type of leadership style.

Another study reports that only 4% of an organization can inspire it's employees. Then it is logical to assume that this 4% comprises of the most influential and powerful bunch of people – the leadership team. However, it is not easy to be inspirational to a large group which is why I explore how we can emerge as inspirational leaders.

Have you ever been through a period of time in your work or personal life where you have felt uninspired?

I certainly have. As a matter of fact, I have multiple times. Every now and then I have this feeling when I sit down to write a blog and no words or thoughts flow for an extended period of time. I cannot generate any worthwhile ideas or even a draft version of a blog. That to me is a sure sign that the fire in my belly has been doused by a lack of inspiration. This may sound familiar to you, either in your own personal case or you may have seen it happen with someone you know. There are many barriers that block you from becoming inspired. These include fear, self-doubt, a distracted mind, low energy levels, and laziness.

According to author Steven Pressfield (Art of War) there is a force warring against your creativity always. It is called "Resistance" and its main aim is to keep your self-worth at its lowest ebb. The second barrier according to writer Anne Lamott (Bird by Bird) is what we call writer's block. Whenever you are feeling uninspired, you are either spiritually or emotionally empty. You need to recognize the difference between being blocked and being empty. So when you are empty, all you need in a refill. Recharge or refresh or rejuvenate yourself.

How do you do this?

To get the answer, you first need to know what inspiration is. The dictionary defines it as "the process of being mentally stimulated to do or feel something, especially to do something creative". I have my own version which says "being unstoppable in the face potential failure, with no evidence that you will succeed".

Advise like "this is just a temporary phase" or "this too shall pass" do not work at all. Just like there is no "magic pill" to make you healthy instantaneously, there is no "magic wand" that will instantly inspire you (at least that I know of).

The real good news is that inspiration is something that can be generated, rather than having to rely on hope or a change in circumstances. Motivational videos and workshops can act as a catalysts but that too is not a sustainable solution.

Sometime back, I made a visit to a small village near Thiruvaiyar which turned into my muse for inspiration that I had lost. After being unceremoniously fired from my job, I was hunting for a new one for a long time without success. My inspiration and self-worth were far below zero. It was at that state of mind that I visited this place to recapture my spark. Here are 3 things that made my mission a success:

1. Transform the Landscape:

If you can't afford to go around the globe, go around your block at least. Distance does not matter as much as 'difference' does. The key is to be present wherever you go and try to connect with the environment and the people over there. The only thing you need to bring for this journey is your curiosity.

Remember one thing, this travel is for a purpose – to reconnect you with your creative self. So go with a plan to not waste time brooding over barriers but to try and break them down with all your might. During my trip, I did not stay at any five-star resort but it was the best I could find at the location. It had unlimited sumptuous food served at my convenience. All I did was eat and talk to the locals about their life and work, and suddenly the flow of inspiration came back to me.

2. Engage with Inspired Future-leaders:

I have always loved interacting with college goers. They are a group that is excited and inspired about their future a lot. Their most intense discussion often revolve around which university they should apply to or which company should seek a job in. If you are grown up now, you might find it hard to convince these kids to talk to you, but the point is that you need to be a part of an inspired group. Hit up LinkedIn or Twitter to find this group.

Once you have found yourself in such a group, you should ask about and listen to the stories of your fellow members. Try to connect with what inspires others in their field and how you can relate that to your areas of interest. More often than not, these stories are good reminders of who you are and what you can do.

3. Dream an Oversize Dream:

Most people think that dreams that are near actualization are the most exciting but in fact it is the other way around.

Just like a flame requires Oxygen to burn, our inspiration requires dreams to sustain it. An almost-realised dream does not have enough fuel to keep the lamp burning. That's when it is time to expand your horizon and get to the next bigger dream or simply infuse the current dream with a greater sense of purpose or intent.

In one of my group coaching sessions for college students, I asked a very basic question and the group suddenly went silent. The question still hung in the air "What is that big dream your harbour deep inside of you?" It seemed like a very simple and straight question to me but the group had no answer.

Slowly the answers trickled out – "I don't have a dream like that at all" "I have forgotten to dream now because of intense exam pressure" "I never sleep enough to to actually dream". This brought me to the understanding that dreams can get lost. From time to time, most of us need a refresher course on building a dream or unearthing it from under the mountain of our day-to-day task.

Building a dream takes effort, faith and hard work, and it is not for the light-hearted.

This brings me to a pasuram from Thiruppavai [Andal or Nachiyar] which powerfully explains how you must awaken from slumber.

மாரி முலைமுழஞ்சில் மன்னிக் கிடந்துறங்கும் சீரிய சிங்கம் அறிவுற்று தீவிழித்து வேரி மயிர்பொங்க எப்பாடும் பேர்ந்துதறி மூரி நிமிர்ந்து முழங்கிப் புறப்பட்டுப்

[Thirupavai #23: Translated - Just as the majestic lion (Seeriya Singam) crouching in sleep inside the mountain-cave during the rainy season, on becoming awake, opens its fire-emitting eyes,(looks all around as the King of beasts), sizes vigorously the locks of hairs of its fragrant manes standing erect, shakes itself up, gets up majestically, comes out of the cave with a loud roar]

I want you all to get up and roar like a lion. Inspiration is very contagious and will spread across your surroundings. It is a great tool which will help you release the locks on the barrels of productivity and efficiency.

Now with inspiration in your mind (and heart) the next thing you need is a clarity of thought. The best way for a leader to have clarity of thought is by talking to himself. Don't worry, this isn't a sign of craziness. Talking to yourself not only relieves pressure and brings clear thoughts to you, it also makes you reevaluate and make smarter decisions.

Converse, chatter, and communicate respectfully with yourself. It is not a sign of insanity. It is a sign of clarity.

Self Talk

Effectiveness of Talking to Oneself

"It's so funny, we don't talk anymore", 'Oh!!! Train journey is a bore". "I don't know who my neighbours are, or even if there is anyone?"

These are not movie dialogues or catchphrases from a book but a summary of today's generation who are forgetting the essence of life and its most important human skill - TALKING. Back in my generation (shows my age - I've hit the time where I've started telling stories of my childhood as a different era) the running jokes used to be on how women never stop chatting and gossiping. This might still exist, but the modus operandi have changed.

Today's conversations are all about WhatsApp, Facebook, Slack et all

- we simply do not talk anymore with each other. We send SMSs. We email. We post on Facebook. We tweet on Twitter. And it is destroying our ability to effectively communicate in our work relationships, in our marriage, in our social life, in our relationships with our friends and our immediate and extended families. Everybody in today's world has a very strong opinion on every subject under the sun - we shout it out to the world from behind a curtain called the Internet. We vent without ever having spoken to a person, without having a real conversation.

We are turning into cowards in the real world like the famous Tamil saying "வீட்டுல எலி இன்டர்நெட்ல புலி" [Translated: Like a rat in the house and tiger in the outside Internet world]. After evolving over hundreds of thousands, we are all trying to find ways to avoid the precious and priceless art of conversation.

An important caveat here is that conversations must never be confused with communication. They are very different from each other.

Nobody talks anymore. Nobody listens anymore. We have allowed these gadgets, phones, and devices to ruin our ability to explore, be intimate and connected with other people.

For some unknown reason, society has made talking to yourself seem weird. Don't be afraid to talk to yourself. As I touched upon in a previous chapter, talking with yourself means you are CONNECTED with yourself. It means you are thinking, reflecting, and expressing yourself, which are all HEALTHY. When you converse with yourself, you can explore your own thoughts, emotions, and behaviors.

Let us assume that you are a chatterbox. Have you ever wondered who listens to your chattering the most? It is YOU. Our internal conversations are what manifests on the outside as our characteristics.

These conversations we have within ourselves define how we view the world, relationships, achievements, success and failures, and ultimately our happiness index.

So it is very logical that if we have a positive conversation on the inside, the outside self will be very vibrant and happy. Suppose if the internal dialogue focuses on your faults, mistakes, weaknesses, insecurities, fears or other negative things, it will be virtually impossible to feel good about yourself and take your life forward. Furthermore, negative thinking can have a detrimental effect on your health and overall quality of life.

On the other hand, if you concentrate on your strengths, blessings, successes, opportunities and other positive thoughts, you will feel great about yourself. You will enhance your ability to overcome obstacles and as a whole, your life will become more enjoyable and fulfilling.

Let me see if I can help you understand the logical reasoning behind why you should talk to yourself more.

1.

To process and sort out your thoughts, feelings and emotions and channelize the outcomes.

When a single thought comes, it always comes with fringes attached to it and hence you need to clearly understand and sort out the core message from the information flow. So talking to oneself is a required process.

2.

Sort of internal issues that you may have before someone else points it out

We need to talk to ourselves to identify the emotions, triggers, feelings, adjustment for these feelings, the root cause for the issues.

3.
Expressing yourself without judgmental thinking

Talk to yourself without judging yourself. You can only do the best you can with what you have. Being judgmental makes provision for biases to enter. So refrain from it.

4.
Mostly to motivate and inspire yourself

Haven't you seen those tennis players who shout at themselves, clench their fist and keep talking to themselves during a time-out? They do this to give that pep talk needed for you to move forward. Give yourself a pep talk if needed: Say what you WANT, and include WHY and HOW you are going to do it.

5.
Practice saying what you want to say to others

Rehearse what you're going to say to others, think of possible responses that might occur. This is particularly useful before going to an interview or a seminar discussion. Nothing is extempore (except certain elements). Most parts are well rehearsed before delivery. This can even include stand-up comedy.

6.
Questioning yourself before committing to any of your actions

It's always good to ask yourself WHY you want to do this. What is the motivation for this decision? It helps you have a clear and positive mind which is one of the most elements for success.

Now you must be wondering if It is really possible to control what you think and channelize your thoughts. The great news is that you can. You can also replace any negative thought with a more positive and productive affirmation. Like anything else, it takes time, effort and tons of practice but I promise it gets easier.

Be Aware of Your Internal Conversations

The first step towards improving your positivity is to really LISTEN to your self-talk. Are your thoughts positive or negative? Do they lift up your mood or bring it down? Are they helping you calm yourself down or are they making you more stressed? Is it helping you or impeding your actions? Unless you consciously try it , you will not be aware when the negative thoughts pop up in your mind. When you start to recognize the negativity, take a break and analyze the situation before acting.

Each day try to make short notes of all your important thoughts and at the end of the day try analyzing it to see how your thought process works in different situations.

Take control of your thinking

If you catch yourself thinking negatively, you can stop your thought process mid-stream by literally saying to yourself "STOP!" Saying this aloud will be powerful and will make you more aware of the frequency and circumstances of these negative internal conversations.

Researchers have found that by saying 'STOP' straight after a negative thought has helped people to manage frustration, overcome nerves, sleep better and stop dwelling on worst case scenarios. You may not be able to control the first thing that pops into your head, but you can certainly control the second or third one. Saying 'stop' is a good strategy that allows you to proceed with more helpful thoughts.

குறள் 596: உள்ளுவ தெல்லாம் உயர்வுள்ளல் மற்றது தள்ளினுந் தள்ளாமை நீர்த்து.

[uLLuva thellaam uyarvuLLal matradhu thaLLinunh thaLLaamai neerththu]

Meaning: Whatever you ponder, let your aim be lofty still, Fate cannot hinder always, thwart you as it will.

Every time I catch myself having negative thoughts, I tell myself this - "I have done what I can do best, I cannot change the past. The longer I think of this situation the more pain it creates for me. So let's chuck this thought NOW". Then using my self-control I intentionally change the subject. But let me also confess that I need to repeat these words more than 20 times before it actually stops, and even that is temporary. So I need to repeat this step every time negative thoughts come back to haunt me again. There is no better way to get out of this situation.

Let me encourage you to start being aware of your self-talk. Determine which conversations are helpful and which ones are harmful. Take control over your thoughts and you will watch your life blossom before your eyes. Remember we are all humans and hence are error-prone. We all make mistakes, we all have shortcomings and weaknesses, we all have some setbacks in life, we experience negative feelings, bad things do happen. The key is to learn from every experience and to exercise self-control to stop negatively thinking about them.

Sports psychologists recommend that an athlete who continually practices positive self-talk will improve his/her performance in that sport, more than by just working on his skills beyond a certain point. Many tennis & basketball players today have successfully put this theory into practice and have seeing tangible rewards.

So don't wait to start talking to yourself.

If you have crossed this step and are used to talking with your-self then there might be another possible roadblock which is communicating with others. There are lots of barriers that may prevent someone from communicating effectively with others. Let see that part of the spectrum too.

Obstacles to effectively connect with people

"The ability to connect with others is crucial for your influence and your leadership ability"

Most people would agree that communication between two individuals should be simple. It's important to remember that there are differences between talking and communicating. When you communicate, you are successful in getting your point across to the person with whom you are conversing. When you talk, you tend to erect barriers that hinder your ability to communicate.

To lead a team to achieve a common goal, effective communication is required. If the leader lacks effective communication skills, it immediately impacts his credibility. If the lack of credibility is not addressed appropriately and immediately. The team will slowly start to dilute the commands from the hierarchy. Eventually, this leads to the failure in achieving the common goal. It is therefore imperative that leaders should possess good communication skills.

Nothing good comes easily, and thus effective communication has its own bridges to cross. They are:

Barriers to Connect

Filtering:

The distortion or withholding of information to manage a person's reactions. Some examples of filtering include a manager who keeps his division's poor cost reduction figures from his boss, the vice president, fearing that the bad news will make her angry.

Selective perception:

This process is often unconscious. Small things can command our attention when we're visiting a new place—a new city or a new company. Over time, however, we begin to make assumptions about the way things are on the basis of our past experience.

Information Overload:

Messages reach you in countless ways every day. Some are professional—e-mails, and memos, voice mails, and conversations with your colleagues. Others are personal—messages and conversations with your networking connections. Add these together and it's easy to see how we may be receiving more information than we can take in. This state of imbalance is known as information overload.

Credibility:

Can derail communications, especially when humor is involved. Have you ever told a joke that fell flat? You and the receiver lacked the common context that could have made it funny. Sarcasm and irony are subtle, and potentially hurtful, commodities in business.

Semantics:

Words can mean different things to different people, or they might not mean anything to another person. For example, companies often have their own acronyms and buzzwords (called business jargon) that are clear to them but impenetrable to outsiders.

Words can mean different things to different people, or they might not mean anything to another person. For example, companies often have their own acronyms and buzzwords (called business jargon) that are clear to them but impenetrable to outsiders.

Common wisdom tells us that being open, approachable, and authentic are key to connecting. It's also critical that you listen well. Yet in the words of Brendan Burchard, "Common wisdom is not always common practice."

திருக்குறள் (Thirukural) – Verse#785
முகநக நட்பது நட்பன்று நெஞ்சத்து;
அகநக நட்பது நட்பு.

[Translated: A smile on the face does not make a friendship; a smile in the depths of the heart does.]

We might assume that we are open, friendly and an easy person to communicate with, but without our knowledge, we might be sending out signals that don't always foster effective communication. John Maxwell suggests that there are four main barriers to communicating and they are outlined below.

1) Assumption: I already know it

It's been said that the three most limiting words in the English language are "I know that." After all, if you already know — why listen? The person talking will likely not feel listened to, even if you pretend you are interested.

In case if everyone thought the same way then there would be no conversation between anybody and only a collision of random words. Thanks to electronic gadgets which is already killing spoken communication in today's world we don't need one more scenario which does the same.

Certain people would like to be left alone, so they display an attitude of 'I won't listen to what you say'. Others might be extra social or even clingy. To overcome this situation of a listener who has the "I already know it" mindset, it is always better to communicate according to the listener's need. Request the listener to spell out what they need and give them back only that data and nothing more.

2) Arrogance: I don't need to know

This is a sure-fire way to make someone feel dismissed, disrespected, or disregarded. The result is likely to be anger or a feeling of being diminished, rather than a feeling of being connected. You need to take extra care when you are speaking to someone who is lower than you in rank or in social strata.

Even though you never meant the words or the tone, the perception of the listener is going to add your position, your previous experience with that person, your command over the community etc. into the current context. Hence you must try to avoid taking a commanding or authoritarian approach.

The sender should take care that the tone of the message should not injure the feelings of the receiver. As far as possible, the contents of the message should be brief and excessive use of technical words should be avoided.

3) Control: I don't want others to know

There was a time when knowledge was power. That time has long since passed! Withholding information will breed mistrust rather than connection. I remember the time when I was in junior high school and the first few rank holders usually use to hide some important information from the rest of the class for the sole aim of maintaining their place in the top ranks of the class. It worked back then, but I doubt it will today.

With the advent of computers and the internet, information has reached every tiny bit of space available on earth. Today what matters is how much information you can share. The more you share, the more power you get. This is the sole reason for the success of social media platforms like Facebook and Twitter.

Since there are abundant mediums today, a leader should choose his mode of communication appropriately. Simple messages should be conveyed orally through ace to face interactions or meetings. Written communication should be reserved for complex messages. Important events and discussions warrant written reminders like Memos, Notices etc.

4) Indifference: I don't care to know

This has a similar effect to arrogance. "I don't care to know" can be far too easily interpreted as "I don't care about you." Indifferent attitude always takes you away from reality and leads to failure.

Even if you have no intentions of connecting with a person, common courtesy calls for completing conversations in a manner that does justice to the other party. Never show that indifference in your words or actions until the person has left the scene.

It is also important to use body language effectively. Displaying excessive emotions while communicating might cause the receiver to misinterpret the intent of the message being delivered. For example, if the conveyer of the message is in a bad mood allows that to seep into his mannerisms, the receiver might think that the information being delivered is not good.

So what else gets in your way when it comes to connecting with others? Time for some much needed introspection, especially in this era of technology. Armed with what you have read through so far, I'm sure it'll get easier.

As a leader, you may have many passions to talk about and would like to follow them. However, they may not necessarily lead to success. This is what Mark Cuban said at the Amazon Insights for Entrepreneurs series "One of the great lies of life is 'follow your passions," says Cuban. "Everybody tells you, 'Follow your passion, and follow your passion." It's bad advice according to him and you are going to find out why.

Mark Cuban's Advice on Passion

Passion is a buzzword in today's corporate world but everyone has a different, (I wouldn't say wrong) understanding of what this means. Passion doesn't imply that you dump your job and start making crafts and arts or dive into photography as your goal. This will not lead to gainful, meaningful or sustainable life. Passion means infusing some inspiration into your job or business that will help you carry it out with happiness and contentment.

The other misconception that many have is regarding what it means to follow your passion or dream. First off, it is not very easy to find your passion and secondly, it is even harder to know exactly when you are ready to pursue your passion. If you are capable of fulfilling your basic needs such as food, clothing and shelter along building a happy family unit, you can say that ready to go.

How to find your passion?

The logical starting point is to find your passion. How do you do it?

There's no expiration period for finding your passion. It doesn't matter if you are 40, 50, or even 80 – what's important is to keep an open mind that keeps discovering things about yourself, as a continuous process. Start at the most basic level. Few questions to help you are listed as examples:

- When do I forget to look at my phone?

- What were things I loved to do as a kid?

- What would I do if money didn't matter?

- What place makes me feel secure and happy?

- If someone took care of all the risks of my actions, what will I do first?

As an executive & life coach, I help a lot of ambitious solopreneurs use their strengths and knowledge to pursue work they love. To do this, I encourage them to share their inner feelings and try to locate that unique thing that not only lights them up but is also beneficial to the world around them. In doing so I have found many myths around the "Follow your passion" advice.

- Myth#1: Passion is all it takes to create success

- Myth#2: Executing the work you love starts with following your passion

- Myth#3: One day you will arrive at your passion

- Myth#4: Once you know your passion, you will never doubt your direction

- Myth#5: Passion leads to your happiness

- Myth#6: You won't make money following your passion.

- Myth#7: Pursuing your passionate work sometimes seems to be selfish

Recent studies from psychologists at Stanford and Yale-NUS (a collaboration between Yale University and the National University of Singapore) show that advising someone to find their passion may not be the best idea. They don't discourage you from pursuing the things that you're passionate about, but emphasize that you should view the idea of passion more broadly: Particularly, you should remember that your interests can evolve, and that you should expect challenges in the pursuit of your passion.

Mark Cuban's Advice

While researching this subject I found this interesting piece of advice from Mark Cuban. But first let me introduce you to Mark Cuban.

Mark Cuban (born July 31, 1958) is an American businessman and investor. He is the current owner of the NBA's Dallas Mavericks, the co-owner of 2929 Entertainment and chairman of AXS TV. He is also one of the main "shark" investors on the ABC reality television series, Shark Tank. In 2011, Cuban wrote an e-book, 'How to win at the Sport of Business', in which he chronicles his experiences in business and sports.

Mark Cuban grew up working class in Pittsburgh. His father installed upholstery in cars and his mom worked a myriad of odd jobs. He chased multiple random side-hustles on his way to the top, including selling baseball cards, stamps and coins.

Instead of attending high school for his senior year, he enrolled as a full-time student at the University of Pittsburgh where he joined the Pi Lambda Phi International fraternity. While attending the University of Pittsburgh, he held a variety of jobs including a bartender, disco dancing instructor, and a party promoter.

In 1982, Cuban moved to Dallas, Texas, where he first found work as a bartender and then as a salesperson for Your Business Software, one of the earliest PC software retailers in Dallas. He was fired less than a year later, after meeting with a client to procure new business instead of opening the store.

Cuban started his own company, MicroSolutions, with support from his previous customers from Your Business Software. MicroSolutions was initially a system integrator and software reseller. The company was an early proponent of technologies such as Carbon Copy, Lotus Notes, and CompuServe. One of the company's largest clients was Perot Systems. In 1990, Cuban sold MicroSolutions to CompuServe—then a subsidiary of H&R Block—for $6 million. He made approximately $2 million after taxes on the deal

One thing Cuban did not do? Follow his passion.

So what is his advice for success, let's see

"One of the great lies of life is 'follow your passions'," says Cuban as part of the Amazon Insights for Entrepreneurs series. "Everybody tells you, 'Follow your passion, and follow your passion'."

Cuban says that's bad advice because you may not excel at what you are passionate about. (Here is the video of that talk - https://www.youtube.com/watch?v=vZvwE5lk-7I)

He added that "I used to be passionate to be a baseball player. Then I realized I had a 70-mile-per-hour fastball when the average major league pitchers are in the range of 90-plus miles per hour. I used to be passionate about being a professional basketball player. Then I realized I had a 7-inch vertical." Top contenders for the NBA draft in 2017 each had a max vertical leap over 40 inches.

"There are a lot of things I am passionate about. A LOT" says Cuban. My take on this too is very similar to Cuban's thought process. What you perceive as your passion does not ensure your proficiency in that area. For example, one of my passions is to eat and prepare tasty food but this does not ensure my success in the hotel business. Who knows, maybe if I started to work as a chef I might tire of it in 3 months. The most important problem with passion is that it changes in a man's life from time to time, it is very difficult to find that innermost and non-changing passion in oneself.

Mark Cuban insists on paying attention to those things that you devote time to. Double down your investment there.

"The things I ended up being really good at were the things I found myself putting effort into. A lot of people talk about passion, but that's really not what you need to focus on. You really need to evaluate and say, 'Okay, where am I putting in my time?'" says Cuban.

The message which I gain from the above statement is that you will get satisfied and enjoy something only when you are good at it. If you can put in enough time, you will get truly good at it. (Similar to the 1000 hour rule of Malcom Gladwell) Nobody quits something they enjoy or they are good at. "I am going to give you one other secret: The one thing in life that you can control is your effort," says Cuban.

The billionaire is not alone in his advice.

"Follow your passion" translate into following your hobbies. (Yes I am generalising here) Let us assume that someone likes kite flying. That doesn't mean that he needs to start a kite flying business. If he did that he would only have ruined one of his hobbies.

Passion is something that you can pursue in addition to your professional life. This myth that you need to work only on your passions to ensure success needs to be broken. People like Mandolin U. Srinivas. Sachin Tendulkar, Crazy Mohan and Kamal Hasan are the lucky outliers. They are in the same field as their passion but we must also know that we can have only one of their kinds.

So let's try and stop looking at passion as a route for success and try to put our focus on our effort.

This shloka from the Gita [Chap: 2 Verse: 47] perfectly sums things up

कर्मण्येवाधिकिारस्ते मा फलेषु कदाचन।

मा कर्मफलहेतुर्भूर्मा ते सङ्गोऽस्त्वकर्मणि॥ २-४७

Karmanye vadhikaraste Ma Phaleshu Kadachana,
Ma Karmaphalaheturbhurma Te Sangostvakarmani

Meaning: You have the right to only work, never to its fruits. Let not the fruits of action be your motive, nor let your attachment to inaction

Now that I have busted the myths about passion then you would be immediately thinking about your next move. Am I going to succeed or fail? What should I do now? My question to you is why you are so afraid of failures and always worried about the unknown. The world and nature runs perfectly on one constant – Change.

If you are not able to adapt to changes and willing to take a few calculated risks then all you are left with is worries and negative thoughts. So start trying to shed these feelings and start taking failures and risks in your stride.

Let us try to stop being afraid of failures. Leaders should never be averse to risk or failure. All of us have that strength to fight the fear of failure, it is just that the current education and corporate system has made failure a bigger villain than it really is.

Avoid Fear of Failure

Ever since monkeys became modern men, 'success' has been declared as the most coveted and desirable emotion. No one enjoys being termed as a loser. We have all been brought up with this belief and have been taught to view failure differently than success. Take the case of something as innocent as a family games-night.

Most of us do not want anyone we know or care about most to lose in anything. This is possible only as long as we do not compete against each other, but the world does not work that way. This creates that heightened fear of failure in all of us. It can be so strong that avoiding failure eclipses the motivation to succeed. Insecurity about doing things incorrectly causes most of us to unconsciously sabotage our chances for success.

Fear is good to a certain extent. It limits the number of risky options or decisions, keeps you on track with the allowed protocols. However, when there is excess fear, its negative effects outweigh the positive. It keeps you from trying, creates self-doubt, stalls progress, and may lead you to go against your morals.

Do you know what causes failures?

• Childhood patterns:

Hyper-critical adults cause children to internalize a damaging negative mindset. They establish ultimatums and fear-based rules. This causes children to feel the constant need for reassurance, without which they feel worried and left alone.

• Need for perfection:

Perfectionism is often at the root of this fear of failure. For perfectionists, failure is the most terrible and humiliating experience. And for this reason alone they sometimes stop trying to do simple tasks.

• False self-confidence:

People who are aware of their confidence level know very well that failure is part of the journey to success. Sometimes adults inculcate an artificial sense of confidence when in actuality, their "self - confidence" is very fragile. It is this kind of people who are constantly avoiding any pitfall and therefore never learn any new thing and become risk-averse.

• Over personalisation:

The ego of ours always tries to over identify with failures. It's hard to look beyond failure at things like the quality of the effort, extenuating circumstances, or growth opportunities.

I might sound emphatic but this is important because negativity and a fear of failure can cause you to miss many small opportunities to succeed, loose despite having the potential to win or even lose your creativity.

This makes it very important for everyone and especially leaders to really overcome this feeling as early as possible. As leaders it is often required not to possess negative feelings even for a second.

"Fail fast and often" is foolish advice.

The idea that we should "fail fast and fail often" is just stupid. I understand that "getting it wrong is part of getting it right," as Charles Handy said. But the first one concentrates on the wrong objective. I get a feeling that we have raised a couple of generations to be totally risk-averse.

'Failure is a stepping stone to success' – this is what was we were taught in high school. But never did the school system build an environment where failures were seen as a path to success. Failures were always rebuked and reprimanded. There was only one directive, one right way. This not only put pressure but also removed the ability for introspection.

Coming from this system, how is it possible for us to enter the corporate world ready to "fail fast and fail early"? Even the corporate appraisal system does not evaluate the metrics or data behind a perceived failure. It fails to take into account the extent of concentrated efforts expended by a team that is said to have 'failed' versus one that has managed to complete a fixed goal.

Failure is Not the Goal

The real objective is not to fail. Failure is not the destination but a milestone you can identify only when looking back. The main objective is to make progress some way or the other. The progress can either be to create a multinational company from notes on a napkin or to create a new product from an existing model. The rules of nature and human nature will still apply.

We need to reframe beliefs about our goals. Having an all or nothing mentality leaves us with nothing sometimes. Have a clear vision for what you'd like to accomplish but include learning something new in your goal. If you always aim for improvement and learning, you are much less likely to fail.

How Life Works

If we want to make progress, we need to work in a new way. When we do that, some of the things will not work as expected. When things don't work as expected, our outcome is not the desired one. Many people will call us a FAILURE. --- GET OVER IT.

When something does not go as planned, we need to do 2 things to do to change "Failure" into "Progress". (1) We must learn from what has happened and (2) We must change our current behaviour.

Let me take you back to India's tour to Australia in 2003-04. Sachin at that point of time was a GOD who could do nothing wrong. Yet in the first 3 matches (5 innings) he could only score (0, 37, 1, 0, 44) 82[1]

---

[1] To all Sachin fans, those figures may not be correct since I am typing from the top of my memory. Don't stay with the data, look at the content and message being conveyed with this point.

at an average of 16.4 - a performance that can be considered a 'failure' by normal counts. And came the 4th test, where Sachin scored 241 not out. How could this batsman turn his failure into such a success?

He just did two things, (1) he went back to the drawing board and saw that he was getting out in the slip + gully area playing the cut short. So he decided NOT to play those shots in the next match. (2) He adjusted his behaviour to restrain himself from playing shots on the off-side. What was the result? A classic double hundred with 95% of the runs coming from the leg side. He made the bowlers bowl according to his plan. I rest my case here.

Remember that either in Life, Business or Sports, things are built over a series of prototypes or experiments. The measure of success is not in how many things we got right, it is in the measure of how much we learned, how much we improved and where we finally ended up.

Here is a step-by-step guide on how to overcome the fear of failure:

1. Figure out from where the fear comes from?

2. Revise your goals

3. Start to practice positive thinking

4. Visualise all possible outcomes

5. Analyse worst case scenarios

6. Have a Plan-B to go

7. Constantly learn from whatever happens

The last point is the most important thing which we need to remember. We can fail but if we do not learn from it, we are not going to change the course at all. That's why this step is very important.

In real life there are only 3 failures:

1. Not trying

2. Not learning from previous experience

3. Not changing how you do things based on what you learnt.

Let us shed rid ourselves of these from today. That will be the biggest acknowledgement I can receive for this chapter.

We can now accept that we are capable of overcoming the fear of failure but there will be sometimes when self-doubt crops up. Can someone who has always been wired to fear failure, who has always been risk-averse not able to take risky decisions really change? You are not alone in having thoughts like these from time to time and there are ways to overcome this.

Avoiding Self Doubts

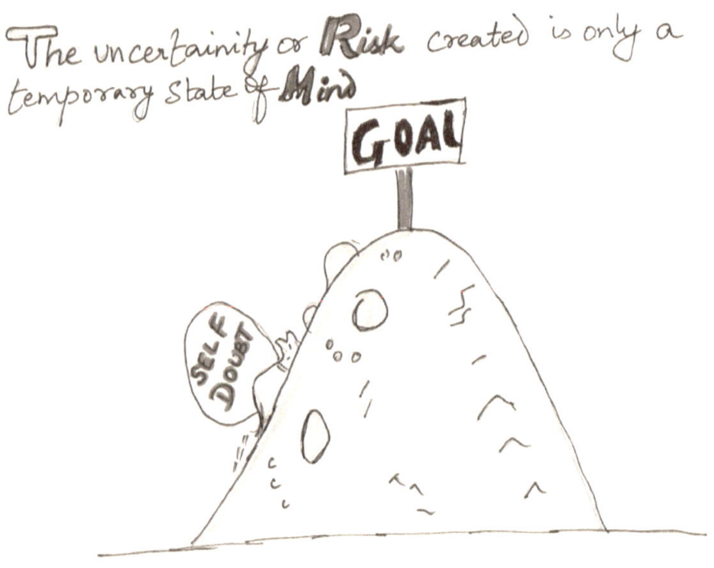

अज्ञश्चाश्रद्दधानश्च संशयात्मा विनश्यति।
नायं लोकोऽसृति न परो न सुखं संशयात्मन: ॥ 40॥

**ajñaśh chāśhraddadhānaśh cha sanśhayātmā vinaśhyati
nāyam loko 'sti na paro na sukham sanśhayātmanam (Chapter 4,
Sloka-40)**

Meaning: But persons who possess neither faith nor knowledge, and who are of a doubting nature, suffer a downfall. For the skeptical souls, there is no happiness either in this world or the next.

What is the way out for self-doubt?

Self-doubt can take a variety of paths to creep into our lives. Generally self-doubt arises from the fear of uncertainty. Since the world is full of uncertainty - from the weather, to your life span, natural disasters and accidents etc. - we are naturally tuned to take these risks into our account. What then creates this self-doubt? It is the uncertain risk factor in our goals.

Some of us are paralyzed into inaction when faced with doubt, this leads the doubt to grow. If we instead challenge the doubt by asking positive questions, then WE will grow. The medicine for self-doubt is so simple yet in reality it tough to follow through on.

First of all you need to be aware that the uncertainty or the risk created is only a temporary state of mind. Yes it will exist only until you take control of the situation. Therefore the more control you take of the uncertain situation the lesser the chance of self-doubt creeping into your mind and blocking you negatively.

At some point in time everyone goes through a phase of self-doubt. You start to think of everything with a pinch of doubt. You normally start with Am I successful? And it then slowly spreads to - Is the money I earn enough for my future? Then it slowly spreads to your abilities - Do I need to acquire new skills? Am I better/more skilled than others in my team? And it continues till you take some action to stop it.

I have firsthand experience with this phenomenon. I have spent more than 40% of my adult life thinking purely about these questions. Just after graduating college I joined a corporate and quickly jumped ship to another one instance of risk with the assumption that this jump would lead me to success, even though it wasn't what I truly wanted.

I held on to dead-end jobs, toxic relationships, and draining friendships because I thought that if I left them, I'd be a termed a quitter.

I doubted myself to the point that I was making my decisions based on what others wanted of me, not what I wanted for myself. I was constantly struggling with confidence and always second-guessing myself. I never knew exactly what I wanted, what race was I running and why I was even running it it the first place.

What I learnt from this experience is that if you do not nip this negative thought process of self -doubt in the bud right away, it leads to total misery. Also it becomes very difficult to reverse of this mindset. In the process of coming out of this loop, I discovered (or uncovered to be correct) few practical and easy methods to overcome self-doubt and build internal confidence. (It's easy in hindsight, yes)

I wish to help you all by sharing the lessons I learnt:

1. Stop comparison with others

STOP comparing your achievements or work with others around you. I found that I doubted myself the most when I started to compare how I'm doing with others. When this happen I get sucked into a vicious vortex of inadequacy and jealousy.

What I found is that the achievements of others are not the litmus test for your success. I found that I feel confident in myself when I follow what works for me and what makes me feel happy/good even if many others think that it is insignificant to them.

2. Don't care attitude

Only when you start thinking and evaluating what others think about you do you start to inhibit yourself. I would like to borrow the words of Mark Twain here - "It is better keep quiet than open your mouth and remove all doubt".

Worrying about what other people think of you will continue to hold you back from doing anything potentially huge. You are better off trying to hold on to your dreams. So at some point of time you have to let go of what others think about you to move forward.

3. History of mistakes

If you have had a failure or a setback if your life, then your mind will prepare to paint all the subsequent decisions with the same brush – which means all the decision will lead to your failure. This is primarily because we fear that we have fallen and it is very difficult to get up and run again. What we need to do is to train our minds to allow us to have some freedom to fall (or fail) and reserve some positive energy to spur us to get up again after the fall. All successful people find an opportunity to learn from their moments of failure and use them as stepping stones to a more successful future.

4. Just decide and course correct on the way

Getting caught in trying to make a decision is the easiest trap that everyone falls into. It is very easy to get stuck in that no man's land of which the 'right choice' is.

So what is the cure for this? Usually when you are at a point where a decision is to be made - the main tip is to go with your first choice since usually that option came from your GUT or INTUITION.

5. Self-appreciate always

A kind word or a simple compliment can bring anyone out of a slump. This is something all of us can attest to. But what if you are alone when you suddenly fall short of confidence?

I have always turned to my own self and have talked to myself a lot. This is a great exercise I found from the movie 3 Idiots. Whenever you feel low - just repeat this wonderful mantra - "ALL IS WELL". It works and calms you down instantly. After you do this, just give yourself some positive affirmations and praises. You will find yourself with your lost groove.

For much deeper emotions and low esteem moments I use this catch phrase - "THIS TOO SHALL PASS" and start marching ahead.

6. Performance anxiety

Have you ever felt like a fraud? Or had success that feels like undeserved? We can sometimes allow self-doubt to creep in when we fear that we cannot replicate our previous success. We may feel that our best has already been created. People can fall into the trap of wanting to replicate previous success rather than learning and building on it. Just try to remember Roger Federer and you will see how he has moved past from this very pattern. Everytime people thought that his best was behind him, he always proved them wrong.

7. Find your biggest fan and nurture that relationship

No (wo)man is an island—meaning you can't do it all on your own. Sometimes all you need is a little reassurance, and your biggest fans are the people who will do just that for you.

First you need to identify your biggest fan - your friend, peer, family member or your spouse - who thinks you are that super hero for that moment. Your biggest fan will be that person who is happy to remind you that you are awesome. We all have people like these in our lives. Put your energy into fostering deeper and lasting relationships with these people.

I've learned that by surrounding myself with my biggest fans, by focusing on my own goals, and by practicing (self) gratitude, I can experience love more deeply and minimizing feelings of self-doubt.

Whether in business or your personal life, feelings of unworthiness can hamper your ability to shine. When we don't perceive ourselves as worthy, we tend to self-sabotage and avoid going for (or asking for) what we deserve.

Everyone has their measure of success, a kind of an internal thermostat with metrics like financial success, professional success, personal success etc. The thermostat uses the basic self-worth as its parameter. The basic premise is that when someone praises you and tells you that you are talented, your self-worth kicks up a notch for a while before returning to its default setting.

That is the reason why you as a leader needs to make your self-worthiness higher for your success. How do you plan to do it?

Valuing oneself more increases their success

Why is it so important to value yourself?

Self-worth.

Self-confidence.

Self-esteem.

These have been three BIG words that eluded me for a very long time. There was a time when I was hurtling towards rock bottom and had failure was written all over me. It was at this point when my mentor told me to sit back, relax and take time off to think about yourself. He posed some important questions to me - Who you are? What are your strengths? Why are you valuing others more than yourself?

These questions led to an ultimate realization in me - I recognized that I was lost. I recognized that the next logical step was to build my self-confidence and esteem. It then dawned on me that we are all change agents on this planet.

If we are ALL change agents, why is it so important to value yourself?

Research has found that to be successful we must regard ourselves with high value. Only then will our words or actions be accepted by others. Unfortunately, there are many times during the course of our life that we undervalue ourselves.

- Here is how you know you are doing it too. Do you.. - Make excuses for bad behaviour

- Hope to change someone despite the red flags

- Sacrifice much more than your fair share or what is expected of you

- Allow people to treat you like a "Doormat"

- Spend money to have someone hang out with you

If you have made checks on this list, it's time to make a change.

We have always been taught not to be selfish, which is true and good value to possess. Yet we also need to understand that thinking about yourself is not selfish. [Read one of my earlier blog on Taking Care of Yourself Is Not Being Selfish]

One of the biggest myths we feed into is that making our own wellbeing a priority is selfish and unkind. The truth is that only by loving ourselves can we truly love and care for others. When we are in good space and are filled with good energy, others around us benefit a lot. Yet, we are so conditioned to believe that it is not ethical to put the person who lives inside your heart, body, and mind first.

So is self-appreciation a sin?

Michael Jordan is considered the best basketball player of all time. Yet, he would shyly say that he was ordinary and it is because of God's grace that he is good.

Once, while deposing in court, he had to swear on the Bible that he would state only the truth. The judge began his questioning by asking Michael if he was the greatest basketball player ever. Michael said, "Yes." The judge was taken aback at this overt admission by the usually humble Jordan. Later, he called Jordan aside and asked how he publicly declared himself the best. Michael simply said: "You made me swear on the Bible, I had to speak the truth. I am the best."

This is self-appreciation

And, when you lack the ability to appreciate yourself or accept yourself unconditionally, you end up feeling rejected. The fear of rejection debilitates, destroys and reduces people. Even now I have to pull out of certain relationships in life and work since I have allowed myself to be taken for granted.

So I decided to change my priorities and started to spend some more time only for myself. I had a great feeling thereafter. Like I said before and can't emphasize enough, It is well known that only if you have love and peace within yourself that you can pass the same to others around you.

Making yourself a priority enables you to be a better person, not just for yourself, but for the relationships your forge along the way. The choices we make from a more loving space is far more beneficial than the ones you make from a place of guilt or inadequacy. Below are seven ways to start valuing yourself and treating yourself with importance:

1. STOP COMPARING YOURSELF

Comparing yourself with others is a losing battle. Doing it only leaves you with a feeling that you lack something. When you are comparing, unless you put yourself in that person's shoes and view life with their parameters and feel their experiences, you are not comparing with accurate data. Most importantly when you compare, you are shifting the focus from yourself onto someone else.

So start shifting the focus back on you and see what is going well for you. Have the courage to pay attention to the person looking back from the mirror. Let go of the inner perfectionist and start to appreciate your smile, your hair, your talents, anything small or large that you have to offer. Starting to see your value is the fastest way to shift focus to the right place.

2 DON'T SETTLE

Some people stay in a job only for the sake of salary. Some people settle in a relationship even when their heart is not in it. Some of us stay with friends who deplete us because we fear unknown company. Whatever you are settling for, it is not worth the cost. You deserve peace of mind and to be outrageously happy.

If you are constantly saying to yourself, "There has to be something better than this", you are probably right and you should be actively working towards finding it.

When you settle, growth stops and when growth stops happiness dissolves. When happiness dissolves your purpose in life is lost.

3. START APPRECIATING

Appreciate small things such as the bed you sleep on, the juice that you drink, your trip to the office. Appreciate the clothes you wear, the greenery that you see. Really appreciated your significant other and your loved ones. But mostly, don't forget to appreciate what you bring to this world. Start to see the joy you bring to others.

The impact of appreciation and joy always has a bigger ripple effect. Just because you are not aware doesn't mean that the effect is not being percolated.

The more you appreciate, the more goodness will flow into your life.

4. CHERISH HEALTHY RELATIONSHIP

Let go of or at least distance yourself from anything that causes a negative vibe for you.

Find yourself in the presence of people who bring something significant into your life. Make it a point to have at least two people who feed your positive spirit, encourage your dreams and accept you for who you are. No strings attached. No alterations either.

5. LEARN TO SAY NO GENTLY

The core value of humanity is to help others but sometimes we are tempted to go overboard at the expense of ourselves. Sometimes we give more than the other person deserves or we prevent people from learning from their own experiences. Continually doing things out of forced obligation can lead to resentment. Instead, honor yourself by doing what feels right for you.

Allow yourself to say NO once in a while. It is not at all wrong. In fact when you say NO you feel liberated - it means we are saying YES to ourselves and spending your limited resource – TIME - on YOU.

6. SET HEALTHY BOUNDARIES

Having defined boundaries actually helps build respect in any healthy relationship. Believe it or not, by having a boundary you have MORE freedom. How? If have established boundaries, you don't have to warn others, pull out of conflicts, build walls to stop infiltration etc.

Boundaries reflect your self-esteem and your values. Healthy self-respect will teach others how to treat you. When someone tries to push you beyond the limits, it's easy for you to put your foot firmly on the line and not get hurt.

7. FOLLOW YOUR HEART

We always come alive when we do something which is close to our heart or our dreams. Don't forget to listen to the part of you that drives your bliss, and be aware of your idle wants and other little things that distract you. Focus on your purpose because dreams never really go away. They simply get postponed.

Your passion can be a small one or a big one. You can even have a multitude of them. Start listening to those small ticks in your heart and find a way to do one small thing at a time. As you start finishing them, your happiness grows exponentially.

Everything in life starts with you and then ripples to your surroundings, so it only makes sense for you to give all the love first to yourself and then to others around you. By living the best life you can inject these ripples with love, beauty, and kindness.

Now that the adrenaline is rushing and your self-confidence is elevating the next step is to look at increasing your productivity.

Increasing productivity is a major goal for many business leaders, as more productive the workforce is, the more money they can bring. While this concept may seem simple, to fully understand what it means to increase productivity, you must go past the literal definition and develop a stronger understanding of the concept as a whole. Simply put, increased productivity means that your teams are putting out products more quickly or completing services at a more rapid rate than before.

Curious? Then just take a quick peek into the next page

Increased Productivity

Every leader knows the importance of productivity. In fact everyone in this world has a very clear understanding of this word, yet somehow we are always turning to consultants to tell us how to make our teams more productive. You need dieticians to tell you how to be productive and eat healthy, you need connected services to tell you how you can be productive while working out or driving. This means that there is something that you are always missing about being productive.

Being productive means to be able to feel the NOW or present and knowing refers to past data. There is a lack of clarity only in the execution stage.

Benefits of Productivity

What will be achieved if we all became productive at work or in our life?

- Self-satisfaction and clear monetary benefits

- Have more time in your hand to plan other tasks

- Tick off items from our bucket lists

- Find enough motivation to start the next big thing

The word productivity found its initial popularity in the manufacturing industry during the industrial revolution. Once we entered the electronics age, intellectual work also fell under the ambit of productivity. When the team is unproductive, it has a minimal impact in the long run expect on timelines but in the long run it erodes competitiveness completely. This means that there is no way we can catch up with the competition once we slip.

Before moving on to increasing productivity for the organisation or a team let us look at a few basic tips to follow as a habit for a more productive life.

1. Value your sleep time

2. Exercise everyday – both physical and mental

3.Establish a power hour – where only things done that contribute towards your important goals

4. Give your brain some downtime during the day

Productivity has always been the buzz word for any leader. While every leader knows this goal by heart, it is fair to say that many of them misunderstand the nature of productivity or the process of improving it.

Either way, such misunderstanding would create a dip in the morale of the team or negatively affect the chance of retaining the best members. It is clear that strong leadership is required to maintain a productive and engaged team. And inversely for a robust leadership team, a productive workforce becomes a must.

Here are 3 easy tips which can enable leaders to drive productivity:

Increase Productivity and Engagement with a Human Touch

When we mention the word productivity to leaders these days, they immediately fix their thoughts on either organizational tools or digital applications. While tools such as Trello, OneNote or Evernote does give a perception of increasing productivity, we need to understand the truth that the tools are only as effective as the person using it.

As leaders, we must try to introduce the human element into the system for increasing the efficiency and engagement of the team. We must acknowledge the fact that it is the team that is delivering the tasks from ground zero. Hence we must try to empower the team to motivate themselves both individually and collectively.

One effective way to do that is by listening to the team and their points of view. The leader has to facilitate free discussions to help the team air their grievances and bottlenecks. As a mature leader, we must try to empower the team to come up with their own solutions, thus making them part of the decision making process. This increases both the efficiency of the team and the quality of the deliverables which directly leads to increased productivity.

Differentiate between Working Hard and Working Smart

Just like the above point, many leaders confuse the concept of productivity with hard work. They at times solely focus on the former which creates an overloaded workforce with decaying morale.

During crunch times, many inexperienced leaders crack the whip on their team to deliver more output. This is all good provided the team has the required bandwidth. If not, it will just make things worse.

A strong leader in the same situation has a different outlook. He takes actions such as changing workflows or processes, eliminating time-consuming and unnecessary tasks, and breaking down big deliverables into small chunks. Even a small change like this could create a big difference in the output.

This not only improves the productivity of the team but also keeps the morale high and shields the workload levels.

Enable Employees to Visualise the Purpose

We have addressed the importance of employee engagement and empowerment of the team but for sustained productivity, we need another arm. We need to understand the employees' fundamental approach to their work and perception of their role in the organization.

While it is difficult and time-consuming to appraise every employee's mind-set, it is easier to give the higher purpose of the work they are executing and its importance to the company's growth. This makes the employee feel like they are making a tangible contribution to something special. This adds value to the task being executed and gives genuine job satisfaction. Even if there is only a 5% increase in productivity of an employee, when combined as a team, the value will be much more significant.

Some practical ways to elevate the purpose of the task is to first eliminate all unnecessary meetings and metrics collection. Most of the employees view these as frustrating and a hindrance to project related tasks. As a leader, you need to come up with valuable incentives (please do not use Monetary plans, it is detrimental) to tap the vast potential of your team.

Some tips on the soft side of the skill also need to be worked at. I like to call this the 4S approach:

-

Be Supportive: Help your team with clear, crisp and quick answers or decisions. Coach them rather than preaching to them. Induce a more positive environment

-

Be Specific: When asking or giving information, be very specific and precise.

-

Be Sensible: Every machine can be improved by redesigning – sure, but can it be done in one day? Keep the actions real and achievable.

-

Be a Shepherd: When the team agrees on an action, act as a shepherd.

Check and recheck the results. Not all the actions will result in improvement but baby steps will take you there.

Making a team productive or improving productivity is not a simple task and cannot be done by a single person or in a single day. It is a big team effort and whenever you achieve the maximum result, be sure to appreciate and celebrate it.

But there are more challenging (and surprising) bridges to cross. One of them is to know how to connect with industry moguls.

Connecting with Senior Executives

All wise leaders agree on one thing: they wouldn't be where they are now without strong sponsors. It's true that developing positive relationships with the senior management is a game-changer in one's career. However, in a world that requires decision-makers to be available nearly 24/7, the entry barrier is even harder to crack.

Connecting With Seniors is Hard

Connecting with senior leaders is serious hard work, but the task is not impossible. There are a few things you must be aware of to connect with a senior leader successfully. The first thing is to learn how to network like a boss. Before you learn how to do this, you need to keep two things in mind at all times. The first is time. You won't get more than 5 to 10 minutes (if you're lucky). The second is the fact. You're not the first one to talk to them about "the best idea on the planet". To engage with the senior sphere, you'll have to be brief, professional, different, and ignite curiosity (all of them simultaneously).

The work that we do is not a solitary experience: we work as teams. Team dynamics are best when people are comfortable with one another, and small talk is the grease that keeps the wheels turning. Bosses and reports go hand in hand. Your boss wants to know who is working for him/her; so does your team. Small talk allows everyone to know these things. Many professions deal with customers, vendors, and other outside parties. Small talk is critical in such roles, because they foster a rapport. There is an old saying: people only buy from people they know, like, and trust. Small talk serves to turn all three in your favor.

A relationship with a senior influencer in your organisation is like a magic carpet ride; it can take you from point A to B in seconds. When done well, it can have a significant impact but it is understandably intimidating to have a powerful conversation with a C-Suite leader. They are sharp, they are smart and most importantly they are very busy. They have conversations with people far more important than you, who pitch ideas far more interesting than yours.

Do not be overwhelmed though. This is a fear we all have to face it requires a bit of training and practice to overcome. One of the things that can befuddle managers, even experienced ones, is how to make small talk with their big bosses or industry moguls.

When you are talking about someone who has complete authority over you, be it your boss's boss or the CEO, the word "small" becomes relative. Anything involving a boss does have a big impact. A conversion with them is like a double-edged sword. It can bring you great opportunities and quick recognition but the flip side is the fear of making wrong statements that lead to your downfall.

Few useful tips

The best way to guard yourself against these elevator meetings is to be prepared - you need to plan out what you are going to say and how you are going to say. This works well if you know that the person is coming to visit your department or if you have the opportunity to chat with him at an all-employee gathering. Here's what you can do.

Do your homework:

Learn the issues the senior team is focused on or the exact purpose of their visit. Think in advance what you will say to a senior person if you meet him/her in person. Work out a key message about your projects, your career and yourself. This is good practice whether you meet a senior person or not. Finally, if it's a more social meeting, try to learn something about the boss's personal interests — hobbies, sports, or their volunteer activities and try to relate your experience with it.

Be yourself:

When you are introduced to them, make direct eye contact and have a strong handshake. Be relaxed and calm, never open your mouth unless asked to. Feel free to inquire about the company's vision, direction to break the ice. If appropriate, talk about what you are working on and your accomplishments. This is your opportunity to use your messages. Strive to be really brief and to the point.

Read the situation:

Keep speaking if the boss is interested; if not, thank the person for his time and move on, even when you didn't get the opportunity to use your key messages. In some ways, your sense of decorum is more important than what you have to say. Rambling on and on about your project or yourself when the other person is not so interested marks you as lacking in self-awareness. Knowing when to end a conversation is also an art.

Good preparation really pays rich dividends. The reason why I am reiterating that you need to prepare even if you are not aware of any scheduled management visits is to leverage even chance or accidental meetings. Opportunities with big shots do not come often, we need to be ready when they do. The good news is that what works for prepared encounters works even more for impromptu ones.

That is why you should practice your key messages from time to time, use the time while you drive to office or before any status meetings. The exercise will give you confidence that you have what it takes to have a clear and coherent conversation with people in power.

Never forget that senior leaders are people first; executives second. Never forget your own personal abilities. Finally never forget that making small talk can have a big impact on your career.

From Thirukkural#697:

வேட்பன சொல்லி வினையில எஞ்ஞான்றும்
கேட்பினும் சொல்லா விடல்.

Vetpanasollil vina elai yengnanum ketpenum sollaavidal

[**Translated**: Tell him what will enthrall him; but indulge not in useless small talk, even if he desires so.]

Here are some more points that will help you prepare appropriately for such meetings:

Know what to discuss: There are a few subjects that you simply should not broach in front of a bigwig, such as personal anecdotes that hold no importance in the corporate world.

Get your facts right: Make sure you have your facts proper. It would be embarrassing to have a bigwig poke holes in your theories in front of everyone.

Be bold and confident: You need to think twice before opening your mouth in front of the elite boss. Confidence should be clearly relevant in your speech, look and even posture.

Rehearse: Do it once, do it twice, do it as many times you need to be sure about what you want to say. This method enables the right words to flow when you start talking.

Choose non-negative words: Frame your sentences carefully. Articulate the key points as adroitly as you can. Phrase your criticism in a polite manner, and only if really required. Placing your opinions in professional circles require a great deal of tact.

Be punctual: Never make your boss wait. If you are headed for a conversation with the boss, reach his cabin on time. Any delay would be regarded as the disrespect of your boss or seniors.

Read the situation: Keep speaking if the boss is interested; if not, thank the person for his time and move on, you will get a second attempt if not now.

Do listen: Control internal and external distractions. Be present; watch the tendency to daydream. Truly listening to another person is the highest compliment you can pay them.

Always close a conversation before walking away: by using a graceful exit line; don't simply melt from conversations. "It's been great talking with you. I really enjoyed hearing about…"

After establishing a valuable connection with an influential person, you need to be creative enough to use this connection in the most beneficial way for you. Once the connect has happened, you need to move one up in the chain. C-suite people always want and expect more from leaders. This means that you will now have to come up with many creative ideas, process or decisions to stake a claim for success.

What better way to explain how to be creative in taking dicey decisions at crucial junctures than to look at M.S. Dhoni. The legendary last over of the inaugural T20 world cup – nobody could have taken such as bold decision and that exactly defines creativity in a nutshell.

MS.Dhoni's Creativity

The human mind is wonderful to study. I have had the privilege of watching my wife work in highly creative and dynamic fields in her career till now - from designing corporate branding to being an apprentice in CSR relationships, from setting up a clothing business to managing events, from designing logos to brochures. And this is just the beginning, she has only more heights to scale. It appears to me that whatever anyone does, be it engineering, music, arts or entrepreneurship, every day brings new challenges. She can choose to tackle all of these in the same way, but sometimes the challenge makes her explore a wider landscape of unknown possibilities.

The world is full of challenges and opportunities. Creativity offers the potential to tackle these with bright new ideas. Which leads me to the - what is creativity?

Creativity is a thinking skill. It is a component of our problem-solving ability, and the process by which we generate a range of possible ideas, thoughts, and solutions. The greater one's creative thinking abilities are, the greater the number and range of options they can produce. The greater the number and range of options, the more likely it is that one of them will provide a path towards a solution.

How creativity functions

The next question in my mind is how does this creativity function?

Educational researchers who studied how creative people generate their ideas found that it is through one, or a combination, of four methods. The first is fluency, or an ability to develop a great quantity of ideas. The second is flexibility, or an ability to develop a wide variety of ideas. The third is originality, or an ability to develop highly individualized or different ideas. The fourth is elaboration, or an ability to embellish and enrich existing ideas.

Now the $64,000 dollar amount question is do I possess any of these 4 skills?

Many studies point to the fact that creativity is installed in each one of us, and like few features of MS-Office, only when you try to use the feature will it get installed and start working. Creativity is not a default feature but has a setting of "install on first use". So the good news is that once you start practicing to be creative, the features in your mind will expand and allow it to manifest as one of your inherent skill.

Right from a young age, you have been exposed to success and failures via media a lot. You have been exposed to many great artists, actors, comedians, sports personalities, athletes, designers and other creative persons. Some of us may have also had the privilege to work with them or see them from close quarters.

Never have you thought about the challenges that are out there that they have successfully faced and overcome. What separates these successful creative persons from others? That question is of greater importance now than ever before because creative work plays a bigger role in business today than at any time previously. Ask any entrepreneur and they will vouch for it.

The easy answer which everyone would come up with is the wrong one. Creativity is not talent or hard work or inborn nature. All these certainly play an important role but it is not what differentiates successful creative personal and the not-so-successful ones. I like to take MS Dhoni here a case study. [There are many who I can take as reference and they will fit in but I find that Dhoni's name resonates with most].

I think the determining factor is in how these people think in the crunch moments. Successful creatives cultivate a different mindset than regular ones.

Dhoni's Thinking Process

Dhoni's creative thinking process are very evident in 7 ways.

1. He always THINKS BIG

The best creative mind always thinks big - Go Big or Go Home. If they are going to take the trouble of writing a book, preparing a speech, or recording an album, they might as well make the biggest impact they can. Dhoni isn't afraid of the amount of work it takes. He is always asking "What can I do that exceed everyone's expectation?" One still cannot forget the final over in T20 WC Final in 2007.

2. He takes RESPONSIBILITY

He takes responsibility for the outcomes. He doesn't expect someone else to come and make him famous or successful, though he understands that he needs the support of others to be successful as a captain. He owns his work and decisions. When the team wins, he hangs back in humility and when they lose, he comes in front and takes on the fire. [Take a look at where he stands for the post-victory photograph after WC 2015]

3. He LISTENS well

The best in the world do not belong to the know-it-all group. Dhoni understands that being good at one thing(Wicketkeeping, Slog hitting) doesn't mean that he is good at everything (spin bowling or opening). As a result, he listens to others who are more experienced. Ultimately, he raises the probability of success since he has more options and data at his fingertips.

4. He seeks HELP

While the best creatives accept ultimate responsibility for the outcome, they enroll others to help them succeed. Dhoni knows he can't do it alone. As a result, he built a world-class team around him and doesn't hog the credit. He happily shines the spotlight on his teammates. He is constantly asking, "Who else can I enroll to help get me where I want to go?" [Example: Suresh Raina, Ravindra Jadeja, Ravichandran Ashwin]

5. He works HARD

Dhoni is not lazy, he doesn't stop once his job is done. In the real sense his job has only just begun. He doesn't display the spirit of authority. Instead. He rolls his sleeves up and does the work that lesser team members or his peers refuse to do. He is constantly putting the TEAM ahead of HIMSELF. Maybe he got this attitude from his previous mentors Dravid and Kumble.

6. He shows true GRIT

No one's form is constant in cricket. Especially creative minds that are subject to many frustrations, failures and flops. But the best keep going on relentlessly. They don't let setbacks define their course of action. Instead, they keep coming back even when things don't go as planned. Dhoni has done the same at crucial junctures throughout his career.

7. He remains HUMBLE

Dhoni knows the success is elusive and fragile. He knows that he cannot attain it all alone nor can he preserve it by himself. This knowledge has made him more grateful and humble. Though they face the same temptation like everyone to become arrogant, he has understood the dangers of it and has adjusted differently. The best creative minds know that success is elusive and fragile. They work hard but embrace humility.

The bottom line is that you have more control over success than you think. However, you need to develop a winning mindset and cultivate the habit of creative thinking. This is what separates the best from the rest. Learn from Dhoni's experience and try to lift the world cup of your dreams today. Let me know which thinking habit is part of your skill as of today and pass it on to me via mail (refer to the last page).

Yes, when you see or read about Dhoni, everyone gets a little inspired but that feeling does not stay for long. Slowly our lethargy and mental equilibrium will bring us back to our normal state. So now the question arises on how we can prolong this feeling of creativity

I always try to read certain genre of books to maintain the creative feeling of mine at a threshold. I would like introduce you to what worked for me and see if it could work for you too.

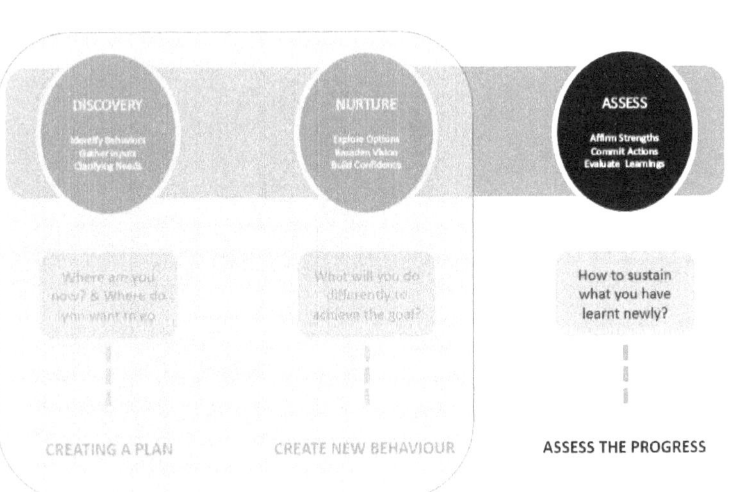

DISCOVERY
Identify Behaviors
Gather Inputs
Clarifying Needs
NURTURE
Explore Options
Broaden Vision
Build Confidence
ASSESS
Affirm Strengths
Commit Actions
Evaluate Learnings
Where are you now? & Where do you want to go
What will you do differently to achieve the goal?
How to sustain what you have learnt newly?
CREATING A PLAN
CREATE NEW BEHAVIOUR
ASSESS THE PROGRESS

Books For Creativity

You may wonder what you should do to keep yourself inspired for longer. The answer is by consuming "outsourced contents" of inspiration. Analogous to the joke about how people trust Dr. Google more than your family physician, you are also more likely to trust the words of others than those of your most respectable family members or friends. Similarly, for continuous inspiration you need to turn to books.

Not all literature is the same, and it's important to have trusted sources if you take this road. This path traverses between 'low energy' and 'early inspiration' and is littered with landmines. On your journey towards becoming a true-blue leader, there might be some days want to be hailed as a boss some when you expect full support for your broken heart. So you should know that you need all of the wise support, which is only available from the outside.

Confidence is like a magnet that attracts people to you and helps you get closer to reaching your goals. When you believe in yourself, you send the message that you have the brains, ability, and talent to handle whatever life sends your way. The truth is, you do! Certain types of books are required to boost your confidence and the task for me in this chapter is to help you find that book.

Ever wonder why many leaders try top give books as a gift? You might wonder where these leaders and up-and-coming entrepreneurs have time for these books. What are the type of gifts they give their colleagues or reference for inspiration when times get tough? Studies have shown that CEOs, business executives, and thought leaders in industries from fashion to food find that books have stayed with and got them all through their tough times.

In this modern age where reading has lost its shine to the ever-changing multimedia gadgets that distract us, I still feel proud to call myself an avid reader who does not endorse any of the electronic gizmos as an alternate source for creativity. People read for various reasons: hobby, recreation, information or to fall asleep. In this age of information, where it is increasingly difficult to allocate dedicated reading time, readers are pushed against the wall to think a lot before opening a book. Is time going to be wasted reading this piece of information? In the olden days, time was spent reading books to cultivate intelligence and creativity, but in today's world the reading habit has changed. Today the expectation is for instant gratification and instant information. I am now going to speak about 5 types of books but to be clear, I believe that ALL books will help you be more creative. I am just trying to narrow things down to help you get the desired results.

Few Genre

We shall start our exploration here:

SCIENCE: I am not talking about the subject textbooks here, those are for putting you to sleep even under the most difficult circumstances. I would recommend you to start reading books which explain how things work in our natural world. This can even include how money works. The value of reading this genre is not in trying to remember theorems or formulae It is to kindle our curiosity or to help us investigate and validate our intuition. Few good examples are The Sixth Extinction: An Unnatural History by Elizabeth Kolbert, and What IF by Randall Munroe.

RELIGION: My take on religion is that it was born with a view to solve many of life's unknown and unsolvable mysteries. If we can try and decode some of them, it generates the best source of creativity for us. By exploring certain unknown territory, we are making our mind work in new and exciting ways. I do not want to court unnecessary controversy by naming one book from a specific religion so I leave it to your discretion.

SERIOUS FICTION: Fiction itself means 'made up'. Imagine how much creativity in entails to create something out of nowhere. Reading fiction creates that feeling inside of us which elevates us beyond our own reality. To name a few To Kill A Mocking Bird - Harper Lee, The Kite Runner - Khaled Hosseini, Catch 22 - Joseph Heller".

COMIC STRIPS: The thing about comic strips are that they state 100% fact in a bloated and exaggerated manner. After reading the 3 blocks of a comic strip, we will find that all those events depicted in the strip have happened to us personally and yet we enjoy them as new and unknown. If we start thinking in the same manner as the characters in the strip, we will find ourselves becoming highly creative. My favourites are Calvin and Hobbes, The Dilbert, Peanuts, and Sad Sack (a yesteryear comic strip).

HUMOUR: The best genre in all the 5 according to me. No genre can kindle our minds more than humour. These books help us forget the Newtonian laws of our world and enter a world of craziness. I would actually advice you read humour in your native language humour than their foreign counterparts. My native is Tamzhil and I read these very vigorously -Devan, Crazy Mohan. Not to leave the English fans in the dark, I adore P.G.Wodehouse, Scott Adams and Dave Barry a lot.

I would like to make a disclaimer that there are way too many books, blogs and sites and secondly I am not that experienced to write completely on my own. However, I presume that at least 10% of those who read this chapter would agree with my opinions or at least start reading to prove me wrong. In either case I would have achieved what I aimed for.

There is no one size fits all solution for inspirational contents. Each one of us are wired to get inspiration from different sources available in the system. The point which I am trying to make then is for us to search and find that one thing which fulfills our needs for inspiration. If not books we could turn to music, videos, travel, adventure games, cartooning or cooking. There are tons of activities and support systems in our present environment. It is the exploration which is missing currently and I would love if we can start it from today.

We usually seek inspiration at a time of stress or negativity. How do we rid ourselves of this stress and absorb as much of inspiration as possible?

According to many surveys conducted by the medical foundations, it is found that most feel stressed mainly due to two fundamental issues. One is economical including lower pay, job security, home loans, equity investment losses and the other is personal relationships including marriage problems, children behaviour, emotional run-downs etc.

How do we combat this?

De-Stressing Yourself

Being stressed out is the worst, and none of us are strangers to it. Between work, family, bills, and other commitments, the stressors in our lives just seem to pile up continuously. And all that stress is just not good for us. Here are the common effects of stress according to experts. Some of them may surprise you.

- Memory problems: If you have been noticing that you are a lot more forgetful lately, your stress levels may be to blame.

- Moodiness: Have you been a little bit more irritable than usual? If you notice it takes less than it should to send you over the edge, it definitely points to stress.

- Obesity: If you have been trying to lose weight but just can't make the scale budge, it might be time to take a look at your stress levels.

• Diabetic: Doctors also warns that too much stress can eventually lead to diabetes,

• Digestive issues: How many times have you gotten some bad news, or had a stressful day, and gotten a sick feeling at the pit of your stomach? Despite what you might have thought, that feeling isn't all in your head

• Insomnia: There's no question that stress keeps us awake at night and doctors agrees that it's an issue.

• Chronic fatigue: There's being tired, and then there's being tired. The latter is what it feels like to have chronic fatigue syndrome, a common symptom of frequent stress.

• Headache: Your body's physical response to stress can often lead to pain, according to doctors

• Hair loss: If you value those pretty tresses, take some extra steps to chill out a bit — or they might start disappearing.

The list is quite lengthy but I think get the point now. It is no use hanging on to the bad things.

In today's world, everything in life is Fast and Furious. Everything involves speed and complexity. Right from your daily news, car, phone, internet, washing machine we have lost patience as a virtue and demand only SPEED. All this speed leads us to a lot of stress.

I can say with 100% conviction that everyone in this world has some kind of stress and not everyone knows how to deal with it. Trying to undo the tension can just add more stress if you take the wrong approach. Many people want to de-stress and few know how to do it well. There are many different ways to relieve stress as suggested by Madeline R Vann, MPH, in an article titled "10 Tips to Help You De-Stress" which was published in Everyday Health. They include:

Get In Motion: Numerous studies have shown that exercising has a positive effect on the mood. The neural chemicals released while exercising helps in rejuvenating the wellness of the body and the mind. By exercise, I mean just do some sort of motion such as walking, jogging, and cycling or even a small game with children.

Get To Giggle: Laughter is the best medicine - an age-old saying is still worth its weight in gold in the present day context. Laughing triggers the release of endorphin, the body's nature feel-good chemical. This chemical reduces the stress hormones and increases immune cells. Thus it improves the resistance to disease in our body. Another aspect is that while enjoying laughter, the mind is distracted from the problem momentarily thus bringing us back to normalcy within seconds.

Get Fresh Air: If you are shut both in your mind and your physical space, take a few minutes to enjoy the outdoors. Go out and get some sun on your skin, some fresh air to blow on your face. A little time outdoors can improve your mood and help you relax.

Get A Variation: Many times, it's easier to solve the problem by removing the root of the problem. In some cases, the root may not be under your control. For example the job in which you are currently demands a different pace than what you are comfortable, or your stress comes from your boss or few co-workers. In such cases, it is wise to change the environment in which you are to solve the problem. Do not continue in the same environment which is creating the stress, it only aggravates it.

Get Decisive: As much as the people close to you may be the problem, not being able to say NO is also a top cause for stress. Saying "NO" when you want to is a very good stress relieving technique. This does not imply that you say NO to all the things since it is important for you to honor the commitments at work, family and social gatherings. Managing your obligations by choosing the correct tasks often relieves the stress a lot.

Get Self-Centered: When situations increase tension levels, it is very normal for the person to put himself as the last priority. In reality, we need to do the opposite - prioritize healthy eating habits, time, and physical activities and sleep, It is better for you to look after yourself first before attacking the problems at hand.

In their quest to overcome stress, people often choose incorrect methods. They include:

- Substance abuse

- Over eating

- Smoking

- Drinking Alcohol

- Gambling

- Anger/Violence

The Tamil Nadu film fraternity seems to show all of the above points as good stress relieving agent. They often depict scenes that appear harmless, but have far-reaching effect on impressionable viewers.

Another point is that it is far easier and effective to reduce stress organically, rather that turn to medication, unless of course the stress in chronic and intense.

Now that you know to handle stress, the next dilemma for a leader is a tough one – decision making.

Imagine that your company has been expanding rapidly over the past 12 months. Sales are up 50 percent, but costs and overheads have also increased and so your operating profit has fallen. Decisions need to be made – and fast! But first you're going to need to consider your options.

We make decisions every single day. Some decisions are simple, others are more complex. So how does one take decisions when the situation is complex or confused?

Decision In Confused Times

There are two kinds of decisions we have to take in life. The first kind where the decision-making is quick and easy and the second one where you find it impossible to choose between alternatives. Some of your decisions are so routine that you make them without giving them much thought. But difficult or challenging decisions demand more consideration.

These are the sort of decisions that involve:

- **Uncertainty** – Many of the facts may be unknown.

- **Complexity** – There can be many, interrelated factors to consider.

- **High-risk consequences** – The impact of the decision may be significant.

- **Alternatives** – There may be various alternatives, each with its own set of uncertainties and consequences.

- **Interpersonal issues** – You need to predict how different people will react.

When you are in the chair to make a decision involving such complex issues like the above, you need to bring your problem-solving skills into play along with your decision making skills if you need your decision to be effective and quick.

There is a generally accepted method or process for decision making which is very systematic and reduces the chances of overlooking certain facts or angles needed for a good decision. This is a very generic process and hence I am just going to skim over it.

The process is:

Create a constructive environment: Decisions can become complex when they involve or affect other people, so it helps to create a constructive environment in which to explore the situation and weigh up your options.

Investigate the situation in detail: Before you can begin to make a decision, you need to make sure that you fully understand your situation.

Generate good alternatives: The wider the options you explore, the better your final decision is likely to be.

Explore your options: When you're satisfied that you have a good selection of realistic alternatives, it's time to evaluate the feasibility, risks and implications of each one.

Select the best alternative: Once you've evaluated the alternatives, the next step is to make your decision.

Evaluate your plan: After all, hindsight is great for identifying why things have gone wrong, but it's far better to prevent mistakes from happening in the first place!

Communicate your decision and take action: Once you've made your decision, you need to communicate it to everyone affected by it in an engaging and inspiring way.

The above process seems very logical and commonly accepted. However, some leaders still find themselves in a conundrum when faced with difficult decisions. It is easier to establish the process, than to think and make logical steps towards implementing it. Hence, as leaders, this is where we fail. I would like to share with you my own personal process, which is similar to the above at its core with some tailored deviations. Let us look at the big picture, the reason for the difficulty in making tough decisions - and that reason is that we are either CONFUSED or CONFLICTED.

Let me look at how the Webster online dictionary defines these two words;

Confused: being disordered or mixed up.

Conflicted: (a feeling of) mental struggle resulting from incompatible or opposing needs, drives, wishes, or external or internal demands.

If we were to analyse these definitions, I can infer that confusion is the result of not being able to think at your usual speed. If you have conflicting feelings, then the result is inaction, over-reaction, or a mixture of both.

Yes, both are possible. We can react strongly to the conversation around the decision, but still not be able to make the decision. The above situation is applicable to both an individual as well as a group. I have to admit (so do you) that conversations with the self can get every bit as frustrating as the ones across the table with the clock ticking against us.

So what do you do?

I have found that by asking a few questions makes the job easier for me. They are -

1. Stop and Diagnose. This is the immediate action which we need to follow. Stop the current flow of thought around the existing process and diagnose.

2. If the feeling is CONFUSION, ask:

Is there clarity on the goal of the decision?

Do you have the right information, and all of it-- or as much as possible?

Is the information organized in an understandable way?

Does everyone involved have the same understanding of the goal and the information?

Do you have a structured process for making your decision?

When you are clear that all of the above have been satisfied, then you're probably dealing with Conflicted-ness. (My spell checker is definitely conflicted trying to deal with that one).

3. If the feeling is **CONFLICTED:**

Then you'll probably experience silence or overt argument. You are likely to see the results from a slightly deeper cause - perhaps at a personal level which needs to be resolved. So whether you are experiencing silence or conflicted arguments:

a) Talk loud and clearly; Say "We have all the required information, the process is stable and established but there is something blocking me from deciding. What is that roadblock?"

b) Remain silent until someone offers a comment: After the first person responds, don't evaluate the remark. Thank them. Allow for everyone to respond without evaluation.

Underlying principle: Until the issue is spelled out loud in the open, it will silently undermine the decision process. Once it's named and acknowledged, it is neutralized. So once it is out in the daylight, the solution will also immediately emerge very clearly.

This step is the toughest in the crowd, since many of us are usually concerned our own issues being discounted, misunderstood, or seen as a blockage to "good teamwork." Yet the person who offers the first bit of truth is the one who leads the group to a more satisfying decision. As leaders, I would like every one of us to be that first guy.

c) Once the issue is on the table, you will see that everyone will offer you more practical solutions, the energy within the group increases and the final desired result in most cases can be achieved smoothly from hereon.

If you are really stuck on a decision for too long, I sincerely advise you to go with the conflicted mode. We usually know the right thing or best thing to do. Facing up to our conflicting wants and needs that get in the way. "Having it all," within yourself whether in a business meeting or personal life, is a decision criterion that can only lead to internal conflict.

So the moral here is: Clear priorities offer the soundest foundation to decision making.

Be clear and take wise decisions.

Most people develop a childhood habit of dodging punishment for mistakes, but it is a habit that must be broken. To thrive as a leader you need to take responsibility for your actions. You need to externally own the consequences for the things you do and don't do. So this is the next step to which you need to act.

Self Accountability

A leader's responsibility is to **share** the **credits** and **take** the **blames**

There is a general school of thought that as a leader we should always take responsibility for everything. I agree with this a 100%.

Is it possible for you to take on such a responsibility?

The answer is yes – we can. The great thing about taking responsibility is that it's empowering. It gives you the ability to avoid feeling like a victim, to own a situation. When you take ownership of your role in any given situation you become an active participant and not a passive bystander.

It is very easy to pass the blame or find a person to point your finger at. Sometimes this may be your go-to response. However in the long run, if the person you are blaming is on your own team, this will only foster negativity.

As leaders, it is our responsibility to share the credit and take the blame. That is what good leaders do. It is a clear sign that you are in control and ready to step up when things don't go according to plan.

How do you do that?

I follow one technique which has always worked for me. I begin to consciously try and take blaming someone as on option off the table. This does not mean that others are not going to be held accountable, it simply means that there will be no blaming or shaming. All it does it take out from critic mode and put you in a mindspace where you instead stick to the facts and try to move forward from where you are with positive or constructive ideas. Try to teach (yourself included) the team the learnings from the mistake and go forward.

There is a very general 5-step method that I want to summarize:

> **1. Own it completely**: "I'm responsible for this situation and I'm on it."

> **2. Disclose it quickly**: speak up right away. This is courageous and clears the air.

> **3. Solve it correctly**: A good solution changes the focus from negative tone to forward motion

> **4. Learn from it thoroughly**: take some time to think through what caused me to make the mistake.

> **5. Get over it appropriately**: Don't beat yourself up, do the 4 steps and shake it off your shoulders.

As a leader, it is important that you take responsibility for collective mistakes made by the team even if your own direct contribution to that might have been ten percent or less.

I remember a scene from the children's movie A BUG'S LIFE in which Hopper (A villainous grasshopper) reprimands Princess Atta (Ruler/leader) who would point fingers at Flik (the inventor ant in the ant kingdom) as the perpetrator of an error. However, Hopper furiously counters with "The first rule of leadership, everything is your fault".

I once had a teammate years ago who was caught stalking a girl on the internet from his computer at work. We received a report from the IT security department of VOIP calls being made to Singapore during night times from my teams' IP communicator. Busted.

Since that was the first time we had run into such a problem at work and the person involved was a very good performer, my manager decided to give him another chance - a solution acceptable within the HR policy guidelines. He was given only a stern warning. Do this again, and severe action would be taken. I figured that would end it.

But NO.

A few months later it happened again, the girl's father apparently has traced the IP phone number back to us. I was the second in command on my team, but my boss was away. It was on me to act appropriately.

I called him (with the HR alongside me) to a meeting and did it by the book. I started with the conclusion: "You've been terminated, effective immediately." I stated the reason: "You were caught stalking a girl on a company compute, bringing her discomfort and unease. You have embarrassed the organization. This is your second offense." And I reminded him that he knew this would be the outcome of his choice: "You were warned that this kind of behavior would result in your termination."

Finally, the HR explained his severance package and told him that the decision was non-negotiable.

But he was just getting started. First, despite irrefutable proof and witnesses, he flatly denied his action. Then he shifted to emotional tactics. "If my parents find out, this will be the end of my life," he said. "All that be on your hands."

All this commotion came down to one simple fact: he refused to take responsibility for his behavior. I realize that people struggle with habits and addictions. Taking responsibility begins with being open to getting the help necessary to overcome them.

Responsibility after a major slip-up

Now what does it mean to take responsibility after a major slip-up?

Here are four steps to follow in order to get you back on track.

Take ownership. It all starts with responsibility. Great leaders display what Joan Didion once called "moral nerve." It takes an act of courage to own a bad situation. It can be terribly frightening to admit a wrong, to be vulnerable and expose yourself to anger and even punishment. You don't have to wait for the absence of fear and doubt. Courage actually means doing it scared.

Show remorse for the problem. It doesn't end with ownership. If we want to turn things around, we have to add remorse over responsibility. Our failings cause difficulty to others. Our mistakes cost time, money, and sometimes heartache. We should express sorrow and regret from the heart for the hurt our actions have caused.

Express gratitude for the reckoning. When a major mistake comes to light, the natural response is to get defensive or hide. But the reckoning is the start of restoration. If we escape detection for a major mistake, the harm is still there. And it harms us even more.

Resolve to take action. Once a major mistake comes to light, it can be easy to slink off and leave the problem in other's hands. In the case of a termination, you may not have a choice in the matter. But you always have something you can do. If you can't fix the actual problem, you can still address your part in it—your failings, misjudgments, destructive habits, whatever contributed to the crisis.

I have seen people walk through these four steps after mistakes just as big—and bigger—than that of my former teammate.

Like the old saying goes, to err is human. But so is rebounding from our mistakes.

What worries us about owning up to mistakes is the fear of negative comments and feedback which we will receive. These days, these repercussions have found a new outlet in the form of social media too. Therefore, when criticism comes to the fore, the senior executives need to be involved in handling the responses with speed, common sense without taking it personally and without argument.

Handling critical and negative feedback is never an easy task. It is imperative that you learn this skill from experienced players. Why should we search for the master when he is always available for us? In the next chapter we will examine one such situation of how Steve Jobs handled a negative comment at Apple's World Wide Developers Conference.

Handing Negative Comments - Steve's Way

Sometimes managers or leaders receive "bad" feedback. Few of us could honestly say that we relish this as a 'learning opportunity'. Some managers will explore and embrace feedback, whilst others prefer to ignore it.

Let us pick a hypothetical situation where a senior manager in your organisation just received the employee survey report for his work area. The report shows that the team is strongly dissatisfied with some organizational practices. How do you think the manager would respond?

Response to Feedback

According to basic management theory, the manager would most likely fall into one of 4 bucketed categories. They are:

1. **THE HURT**: Overreacts to feedback and makes statements like: "My team hates me" or "I might as well resign"

2. **THE HUNTER**: Tries to work out who provided the critical feedback - "I've got a couple of people in my team who are negative about everything." And also look for reasons to dismiss team feedback

3. **THE HIDER**: Pretends the report never arrived and files it away in a folder called "Later". The hider can also use other work priorities as an excuse to ignore survey feedback "I'm too busy right now with X project".

4. **THE HEARER**: Explores both positive and negative feedback with their team and listens to the discussion. Works with their team to identify next steps for dealing with key issues.

Yes – your guess is right, we all need to fall into the 4th bucket and yes - it is hard.

None of us have escaped from receiving any negative feedback be it from our bosses or from our spouse (both create the same frustration and feelings in all) As leaders, we need to be coached to receive them. There are some tips to do this including:

- Controlling your emotions
- Not confusing the behaviour with the person
- Evaluating if there is truth in the message etc.

We are in the world of the internet where insults have become the easiest choice of weapon. Internet trolls are the best example of my point. Competitors use them to throw us off our game. Everyone at some point of time uses insults especially when they feel insecure or threatened.

Job's Way of Handling Negative Comments

We are in the world of the internet where insults have become the easiest choice of weapon. Internet trolls are the best example of my point. Competitors use them to throw us off our game. Everyone at some point of time uses insults especially when they feel insecure or threatened.

Negative feedback is required but insults are not designed for help, they are designed to hurt. There are many effective ways to handle insults and one of the best which comes to my mind comes from an unlikely source: Co-founder of Apple Computers, Steve Jobs.

In 1977, Jobs had just returned to Apple after his ouster a decade ago. He was answering questions for developers at Apple's World Wide Developers Conference when one audience member took a shot at him:

"Mr. Jobs, you're a bright and influential man," he begins.

"Here it comes," responds Jobs, as both he and the audience giggle.

Then, the famous insult:

"It's sad and clear that on several counts you've discussed, you don't know what you're talking about. I would like, for example, for you to express in clear terms how, say, Java and any of its incarnations addresses the ideas embodied in OpenDoc. And when you're finished with that, perhaps you can tell us what you personally have been doing for the last seven years."

Ouch.

For most of us, such a public attack as this one would have left us a flustered. But Jobs's response is a perfect demonstration of what to do in those situations. Here is what he did:

He took a pause (that seemed eternal but lasted only about 11 seconds). (He sipped some water and reflected on the question and the criticism.

"You know," he begins his reply. "You can please some of the people some of the time, but…" Another pause and this time for about 8 seconds.

It is a very well-known fact that Lord Krishna when delivering the famous Gita discourse to Arjuna used a lot of pauses. The pause is so valuable because it allows you to get your emotions under control and think things through before saying or doing something that you may regret later.

He agrees with this accuser - "One of the hardest things, when you're trying to effect change, is that — people like this gentleman — are right! In some areas," explains Jobs.

For many years academics have argued that the best way to change a person's mind is not to attack their position, but rather, to find common ground. Jobs does this perfectly by acknowledging the validity of his detractor on some counts.

He then goes on to make a solid argument by outlining his role at

Apple as not to know the ins and outs of every piece of software but to see the big picture, to reiterate the vision, and to keep everyone on course.

[Quote] "The hardest thing is: How does that fit into a cohesive, larger vision, that's going to allow you to sell 8 billion dollars, 10 billion dollars of product a year? And one of the things I've always found is that you've got to start with the customer experience and work backwards to the technology. You can't start with the technology and try to figure out where you're going to try to sell it." [Unquote]

This extremely compelling vision of working backwards from customer experience may have been innovative at the time. But as history proved, it was right.

He uses vulnerability to his advantage - Jobs admits that he has made mistakes, this is a necessary skill for a leader. Jobs not only explains his vision, he uses his own failed experiences to help establish his credibility. In essence, he begs stakeholders (and shareholders) to learn from his experience.

He praises his people and team - "They're doing their best," says Jobs. With these words, Jobs gets behind his team. He acknowledges them. He praises them. He lets them know he's got their backs. This inspires the team (and others) to get behind him, too.

He finishes strong - as always. Jobs says in his closing comments that people make mistakes and it is good thing - it enables everyone to learn from that experience and move forward with strength.

He then comes full circle to the original questioner: "Mistakes will be made... some people will not know what they're talking about, but I think it is so much better than where things were not very long ago."

"And I think we're going to get there."

Link to the original article is below. (Copyright 2017).

URL: https://www.inc.com/justin-bariso/20-years-ago-steve-jobs-demonstrated-the-perfect-w.html

We have inched our way to the conclusion of this book, having covered all the areas to explore, nurture and assess your potentials, skills, behaviour as a leader. Yet there is one message which I wanted to close with. The reason I started to write this book in the first place. Many of us have a time tested image of certain activities and their perceived level of difficulty. We never seem to test it or refute it. For example: I have never thought that I can draw. I never even lifted my hands to pick up a pencil to draw. I would always admire, appreciate and consume art. But never execute it.

One day when I was really low in energy and self-esteem, I decided to try being creative and started to type out a blog on an impulse. The next day I decided that without some structure, I would lose this energy. Therefore I tasked myself to complete 50 blogs in 90 days. I surprised myself by actually finishing my target in 47 days.

During the course of those blogs, I started to scribble some drawings which to my surprise evolved into cartoons. These cartoons that you see here. They have been made more vivid and perfected by my kids. That was the moment when I changed from consuming to creating.

If you thought that consuming was entertaining then try creating – it is so much more.

Consumer To Producer

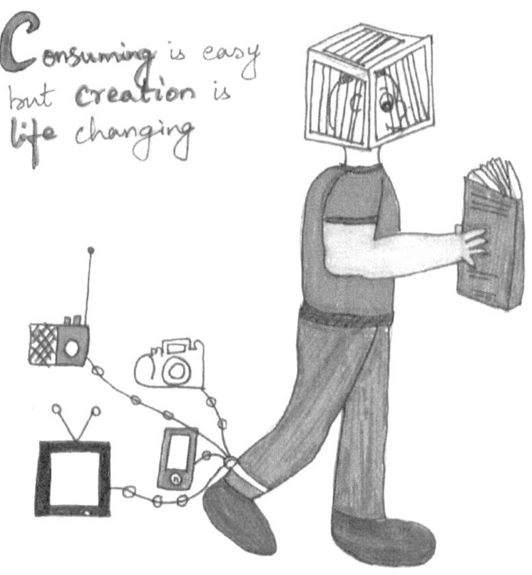

Consumer to Producer - What changes?

"Creativity is allowing yourself to make mistakes. Art is knowing which ones to keep" - *Scott Adams*

I grew up like every other teenager of the 80's and 90's – breathing cricket, reading MAD, watching MTV. I was obsessed with Madonna, and Michael Jackson. I loved all of it; the music, the visuals, the performance. I decided that I too needed to become a popular like them.

Cut to present day reality, I am still one of the insignificant cubicle confined corporate managers trying to find his passion. It was less than a year ago that I decided to start writing/blogging.

Until this artistic awakening, I had no interest in YouTube lessons on creative writing and storytelling because I was convinced that there was no way to improve my skills. When I decided to do my own thing, I entered a completely different ball game. There were no notes to follow, there were no grammar constructs to obey. I needed to decide for myself what the words and the plots were going to be. This required a whole new way of thinking, seeing and writing.

Consuming is easy. Getting inspired is easier. Following instructions is the easiest. But when you go from being a consumer to being a creator, you start to think about things you never thought about before. It is equally overwhelming and exciting. I wasn't always sure I was going to be able to do it. Yet, when I shifted from being a consumer of blogs to a creator, my life changed profoundly.

For the first time, I started to view things I had never viewed before, like narration style, sentence constructs, plot flow and sequences that made me enjoy the piece. How does one really convey controversial or unfavorable opinions without hurting others? For the first time, I started to really appreciate the power of conveying a message, and the huge part that played in creating a motivational blog. How had I never cared for it before?

I started to pay attention to l the different metaphors/anchors that were being used and it blew my mind. I started watching people, analyzing their thought process and sentence constructs during my travel to office (I use the local train and trust me it's the best source you can get). Writing opened me up to a whole other world that was richer and more fascinating, and I started to appreciate it so much more than I had ever before. It became more organized and multi-dimensional.

Becoming a creator and not a consumer turned me from a being receiver to being a sensor. I have become acutely aware of what is happening around me. Everything now has become potential material in my creative pursuit.

I became an active hunter-gatherer of ideas. Ideas kept popping into my head all the time. I have now started to carry a notebook (a physical one, not electronic) with me everywhere.

Everything became interesting. Facial reactions to extreme opinions, anti-Modi comments, movie reviews, hating the latest Tamil film songs. I started to collect stories, moments, feelings, anecdotes, quotes, and jokes happening around me throughout the day. I started spotting interesting names, logos, and colors everywhere. My notebook became my favorite thing, my treasure trove.

Eventually, I think I have found my passion (for the present) - to become a famous author. This discovery has not been incidental. It has happened because of this shift.

Becoming a creator has changed the way I see everything in life. The world is so full of content that it is easy to sit back and just consume it. Creating is hard. It quickly makes you aware of your shortcomings and your lack of knowledge. (I have to research at least 7-8 blogs to start writing the first paragraph on a motivational topic)

Yet, moving from a being consumer to a creator in every area of life will open your eyes and your senses to so many fascinating things. Everything is a story. Everything can be a seed for an idea. You will become infinitely curious about life. The world will become richer, and a more interesting place to be. What a beautiful way to move through life, don't you think?

As a challenge to break my internal stereotypes, I have decided to read the book named "Drawing on the Right Side of the Brain" by Betty Edwards. I have always maintained that I cannot draw. Painting came to his highness Raja Ravi Verma, but for me 'Painting வருமா' (translated: will come?) is a big question till today. My next aim to go from consuming good paintings to creating horribly wrong pictures. (I think I am almost there)

All the cartooning that you see in the beginning of each chapter have been skillfully destroyed beyond recognition by my cartooning skills and then repaired to the extent possible by my kids (Son: Vikranth & Daughter: Vismitha). I am yet to finish the book but I feel I that I have evolved from scribbling to weird faces and emotions to creating palatable stick figures. I still trust my writing over my artistic abilities though more on the book than on my drawing gene.

Now here is my challenge for you:

Have a think about all the things that you consume and love. Is it books, music, perfumes, fashion? Maybe you love looking at someone who can dance really well. Or you love eating your mother's cooking. Or perhaps you admire someone who knows how to code, or builds shelves or fix cars, but you have never thought you would be able to do something like that.

Instead of observing and consuming, I challenge you to pick one of these things and try to become the creator yourself. Ask someone to show you the ropes. Spend a bit of time on YouTube tutorials. Join Skillshare. Start with something small and simple.

In no time, you will begin to enjoy the challenge and I am sure you will surpass your goal. There is no better time than now to start creating.

Let me know in the end what really changed in you.

Was this book useful in kindling that sleeping giant within you?

That was my goal and I have accomplished to even a small extent. We have gone over the discovery, nurturing and the assessing part of the journey until now. As a leader, it is now in your hands to deliver the efforts and nurture your leadership DNA. If you are still doubting yourself I have only one arrow left – the last chapter aptly titled "It's a wonderful Life"

It was written as my 50th blog in my 90 day challenge. It has all the motivation that I can give and I hope you receive it with an open heart and mind.

It's A Wonderful Life

October 2016.

Two weeks ago, I was so frustrated with myself that I decided to watch some really old English classic movies to calm myself. When I was searching for options, I stumbled upon the highly rated "It's a wonderful life". I gathered my entire family to watch it (despite their and my lack of enthusiasm). The story unfolded slowly. Half an hour into the movie, I could see myself in the shoes of the protagonist. Every scene seemed to have been taken from the story of my life. It wasn't a good feeling. My wife and I decided to give it a few more minutes and turn it off if it did not improve. It was then that the movie actually started to pan out and by the end we realized how much we would have missed had we abandoned it half-way.

'It's a wonderful life' is a 1946 American Christmas fantasy drama movie directed by Frank Capra based on a short film "The greatest gift". The plot is very simple, the protagonist (James Stewart as George Bailey) gives up his dreams just to help others. Due to many subsequent traumatic events, he decides to end his life on Christmas Eve. The antagonist is on a single mission to block George in all his venture and he uses his entire money to block him time and time again. George is standing in front of a bridge waiting to jump and end his life, but there is a person who intervenes his suicide attempt and calls himself his guardian angel. George Bailey tells the angle that he wishes he was never born and the angel using magic creates an timeline where George never existed to show him what that would have been like. This vision makes George realise how many lives he has touched and helped, and finds a purpose for his existence.

Like this movie illustrated, you truly get real strength and hope just by thinking of how many people's lives you have touched. Whenever you are passing through a rough patch, you need to sit back and remind yourself of everything you have done for others. This allows hope back into our hearts again.

I was tempted to look into our Tamil culture to see if I can find a similar concept and this one struck me in the first 5 seconds of thinking. The words of Kannadasan: *தர்மம் தலைகாக்கும் தக்க சமயத்தில் உயிர் காக்கும் கூட இருந்தே குழி பறித்தாலும் கொடுத்தது காத்து நிற்கும் - செய்த தர்மம் தலைகாக்கும் தக்க சமயத்தில் உயிர் காக்கும்*

[Dharmam thalaikaakkum thakka samayaththil uyir kaakkum koota irundhE kuzhi paRiththaalum kotuththadhu kaaththu niRkum - seydha dharmam thalaikaakkum thakka samayaththil uyir kaakkum]

Translated into English: the charity you do will save your head, at the appropriate time, it will save your life! Even when you have people plotting against you while pretending to be with you, whatever you gave (through charity) will stand guard to protect you!

The word Dharman here is quite debatable and has varied meanings and interpretations but I find in the context of the movie we were talking about earlier that this term can be used to represent 'touching lives'.

What this movie has done personally to me is that it has changed my perspective of how to attack a problem, how to remain calm and sail through problems without disrupting your mind and sanity. This movie served as an apt catalyst to reignite this dormant realization. If you are struggling in a similar position, give this a watch and let me know if it worked the same wonders on you as it did on me.

I was hunting for a topic befitting my landmark 50th blog to touch as many lives as possible. Perhaps it was destiny that brought me to to this movie at the appropriate juncture.

I thank all of those who have patiently deleted all my posts from their social media notifications during by 50 blog posts challenge. I would not have succeeded without the patience of my readers and assistance of family in getting topics and giving my tough love and encouragement.

My success lies not in the number of blogs that I publish but the number of people who have changed or received another perspective from any of them.

I would like to borrow Robert Frost's words from the poem "Stopping by Woods on a Snowy Evening." to end here and say "But I have promises to keep, / and miles to go before I sleep, / and miles to go before I sleep..."

Conclusion:

What is the message that I have passed on to you?

Proposing a new theory about leadership is quite similar to adding a flavour to a Baskin-Robbins menu. Sure, my efforts to introduce new ideas will be appreciated but who is going to buy into a new idea in this already clouded field?

Advancing a new view of leadership, especially one that emphasizes complexity, introspection and the democratic cultivation of new leaders is challenging but necessary. With the industry moving and changing at break-neck pace, the approach to leadership should also keep up. How better to do this than by using our own evolutionary DNA and discovering our true potential.

Leadership, quite simply, is built on the notion that leaders are not born but nurtured through our journey. Across my book, we have uncovered this framework in three segments: a) The discovery or the ability to adapt to changing requirements and complexity (introspection) b) Nurturing or the willingness to put your head down and practice discipline in what you believe and c) Assessing or being honest and vulnerable while staying true to your core values.

When it comes to customer service, everyone in the team is a leader. You do the right thing, because you know it's the right thing to do. Others notice and admire you. Let me give you a quick example of what I mean.

I was with my wife at a five-star restaurant for a special dinner to celebrate our anniversary. The place was truly exotic and spic-and-span.

In a hurry to see the buffet menu for the buffet I gathered some speed. As I accelerated, I slipped (and quite literally fell for my wife) on a puddle of water I hadn't noticed. Two servers who were standing nearby noticed me and smiled at me. I smiled back to reassure them that I was okay. What surprised me was neither of them did anything. I thought they might grab one of the many napkins on the buffet table and wipe up the wet spot on the floor, but they did not.

To ensure that no one else had a similar slip, I asked them to have the spot wiped dry - which they dutifully nodded to and sent for a janitor. Some time passed and no one showed up so I picked up the napkin from my table and was about to mop the place up myself when a well-dressed man in Armani suit beat me to it.

It was obviously not his job, but he did not hesitate to do it. He was clearly a man of affluence, but what I soon found out was that he was also the CEO of the hotel. He quickly gave his staff a quick talk and went on his way.

His hands-on leadership still stays in my mind. It is our job as a leader to do whatever it takes to to keep the system clean, efficient and happy. Cleaning up or picking up trash is a small thing – especially when it is your own trash. Leaders know that little things count. They don't think about it. They don't care if anyone is watching. They just do what's right.

Now might think: if everyone is a leader, then who is going to follow?

It is estimated that in an organization more than 75% to 80% people are always followers who look up to the leaders for direction. So according to these stats are only 25% of people leaders? The answer lies in the question itself. 25% of the time, everyone needs to be a leader and 75% of the time everyone needs to follow what the leader's (the inner self) guidance. Positions like CEO, CTO and COO are limited, but when products or services have to be built as a team or organisation, everyone at some point in the life cycle of the product will have to wear the hat of a leader. At these moment it is important that you are capable of rising up to the challenge of the role.

Hence, I wanted to spread the message that everyone has this potential and needs to work on it. Hence proved = "Everyone is a leader"

At the end, I also want to spread the framework for of Discovery, Nurturing and Assessment without restricting them   to self-development, leadership skills or marriages or creativity. It is a framework with which we can even try solving even larger issues like global warming or world hunger. It just takes the execution of 3 steps with total dedication of time and effort without success on the immediate horizon.

I took some inspiration from the farming community and the framework they operate on, which is SOW, GROW, HARVEST.

The discovery is in finding the right seed to plant, the nurturing is to grow the plant in a stable environment and finally, the assessment is to Harvest the results.

Through the metaphor of the seed I want to explain this:. When you look at the banyan tree and are marvel at vastness, do you ever think for a moment that all that everything that has manifested and in front of your eyes has come from that small little seed. The same applies to your talents. It is all there inside your little mind – you just need to nurture and grow it in the right spirit.

I would like to end here with a closing thought on overcoming self-doubt.

Swami Vivekananda comes to mind immediately when I think of exemplifying inner strength. All his powerful messages came from this inner strength. The Shloka which Swami held very close to his heart is from the Gita - Chapter#2 Shloka#3

क्लैब्यं मा स्म गमः पार्थ नैतत्त्वय्युपपद्यते |
क्षुद्रं हृदयदौर्बल्यं त्यक्त्वोत्तिष्ठ परन्तप || 3||

**klaibyam mā sma gamah pārtha naitat tvayyupapadyate
kshudram hridaya-daurbalyam tyaktvottishtha parantapa**

O Parth, it does not befit you to yield to this unmanliness. Give up such petty weakness of heart and arise, O vanquisher of enemies.

To succeed in life a person, requires high spirits and morale. He needs to be optimistic, enthusiastic, and energetic to overcome such as sloth, ignorance, and unrealistic desire. When such negativity flows into our minds, it is imperative to counter it with positive data.

Krishna here refers to Arjuna here as Parth since Pritha is another name for Kunti (Parth means 'Son of Kunti'). He invokes the valor of Kunti who worshipped Indra and with his blessing, gave birth of was Arjuna. Krishna reminds him of this, and encourages him not to yield to this moment of weakness, which does not befit his illustrious parentage

When negativity gets into your mind and thereby to your heart, that feeling is neither moral nor a true feeling. It is just lamentation and delusion and its main aim is to make your mind weak. If our behavior was truly based on wisdom and mercy, then we will experience neither confusion nor grief.

Swami Vivekananda followed preached the same – shed and conquer the delusion and fear which are your biggest enemies. Once they are vanquished, success will follow you everywhere.

So let not be bound by fear.

May all the gods be with you as you begin a new chapter of your life.

Sri Ramajayam

Thank You All So Much

Every little task that we do is indeed a miracle after it is completed. The writing process for this book took some time and more so an intense soul-searching. There were lots of times when I felt that I cannot cross the line but it was my wife who pushed me all the way. This book is not possible without the help that my family extended. When I was searching for the topic I was not able to really locate the topic or the central theme of the book but was certain it needed to be about leadership.

Then when I stepped back I got the topic by looking at my wife - Ramya. She is such a soft person and is virtually afraid of everything - from a small centipede to a big elephant much like kamal's character in the movie Tenali. When some sudden calamity or a big obstacle comes, this same person behaves in a totally opposite way. She draws her courage and stands to fight the battle. This made me realise that all of us have this leadership skill inside of us all the time and surfaces when needed. This made the central theme of the book. I am really moved to write this book on how many of you can find your hidden skills and what it means to you. As in the movie "It's a Wonderful Life" I will be supremely happy if I could touch a few of your lives through this book.

Whatever short comings in this book and contents, they are mine alone; whatever values that are here are all owed to the contributions of others.

First I would like to thank the almighty God for giving me a wonderful family that have insisted on maintaining the traditions which has helped to come this far. Although I have borrowed a lot of contents from every place that I could touch, the intention of borrowing them was to spread this message - It's inside of you. I am filled with happiness and gratitude to my father, V.N. Mukundan without whom I could never have linked so many Gita Sloka's, the Andal's Thirupavai and the Thirukurals. He has spent many hours with me explaining both the sloka's and the connection to engineering.

Secondly, my best critics were my children (Vikranth & Vismitha) to whom I gave these contents and observed their faces while they read. Often they used to frown saying the chapter is easy to read but what's the central message? So to make them happy I came up with the idea of a cartoon. As my drawing skills are next to that of a two year old, I requested my kids to draw. It was they who conceived the theme, the characters, the colours and the caption line for each chapter.

Thirdly I would like to thank my editor Samitha Suresh who in the name of editing has actually re-written the whole contents. Without her constant help and efforts the current book would not have come to this shape. I particularly loved her way of reducing the contents with such crisp sentences and the swiftness. I would also like to thank my engineering college friends (Sundar & Nandakumar) who volunteered to do freelance editing and did a fair job at it.

Fourthly, I am very grateful to Mr.La.Sa.Ra.Saptarishi who in spite of his stature and age in helping me. He has done all the ground work for this book to be rendered in the physical form single-handedly. Without his total efforts, guidance and directions I am sure I would have been left clueless still having separate pages in my hands rather than the book.

Finally I want to thank my family and cousins who have patiently read all my blogs (think so) for a long time maintaining the same enthusiasm displayed for my first blog. They have been the best fans of me and my major motivation.

References

"The Champion's Mind: How Great Athletes Think, Train and Thrive" By **Dr. Jim Afremow**

"Myths of Creativity" By **David Burkus**

"Under New Management" By **David Burkus**

TEDx Talk **by Emilie Wapnick** (TEDx April 2015)

"Coaching for performance" By **John Whitmore**

Various Internet blogs on Sleep and waking up

"It's Already Inside" By **Robert Murray**

"Making Your Leadership Come Alive" **by Jeremie Kubicek**

Qualities of Inspiration from Psychologists Todd M. Thrash & Andrew J. Elliot research material"

Positive Self Talk blog by **Dale Carnegie**

Good Communicaton **By John Maxwell**

Amazon Insights for Entrepreneurs Talk series **By Mark Cuban**

Various Internet blogs on improving team productivity

Blogs from **Internet**

Blogs from **Internet**

Allthingsworkplace.com

Q&A in Apple's World Wide Developers Conference,1997 By **Steve Jobs**